WIRING
Your Toy Train Layout
— SECOND EDITION —

Peter H. Riddle

KALMBACH BOOKS

Kalmbach Books
21027 Crossroads Circle
Waukesha, Wisconsin 53186
www.Kalmbach.com/Books

Published in 2013
17 16 15 14 13   1 2 3 4 5

Manufactured in the United States of America

ISBN: 978-0-89778-543-3
EISBN: 978-0-89024-918-5

Editor: Randy Rehberg
Art Director: Tom Ford
Illustration: Peter H. Riddle, Rick Johnson

Unless otherwise noted, all photographs were taken by the author.

Publisher's Cataloging-In-Publication Data

Riddle, Peter.
  Wiring your toy train layout / Peter H. Riddle. -- 2nd ed.

    p. : ill. (some col.) ; cm. -- (Classic toy trains books)

  ISBN: 978-0-89778-543-3

  1. Railroads--Model--Electric equipment--Handbooks, manuals, etc. 2. Railroads--Models--Design and construction--Handbooks, manuals, etc. I. Title. II. Title: Classic toy trains.

TF197 .R4923 2012
625.1/9

CONTENTS

Introduction

These trains and transformers were manufactured approximately 90 years apart, but the basic principles involved in their operation are the same. If you were to move each train to the opposite track, the transformers could power them. In the early 20th century, some transformers, like this Lionel model, were provided with extra long wires and screw-type plugs to be inserted in an overhead lightbulb socket.

The wonderful hobby of model railroading traces its roots almost to the beginning of railroads themselves, and it achieved great popularity in the years between the two World Wars and during the 1940s and 1950s. Throughout those years (as well as during the 1960s through '80s, when public interest in toy trains suffered a decline), one basic piece of equipment made running the trains easy: the alternating current transformer.

This device required only a pair of wires connected to the track to convert household power into low voltage current suitable for running the miniature electric motors in the locomotives. Even very young children could enjoy these fascinating toys in relative safety without adult assistance.

A powerful reason for the appeal of electric trains is the opportunity to expand a basic train set into a miniature railroad by adding extra track, turnouts (commonly called *switches*), and various kinds of accessories. Add to that the possibility of running two, three, or more trains, and it isn't difficult to keep interest high. But unfortunately, as a train layout grows in size, and its components multiply, the need for more complex wiring grows exponentially.

One major problem involves operating two trains independently. If two locomotives are placed on the same track, they both receive current from the same transformer at the same time. If the direction button is pressed, both engines will stop and reverse simultaneously. If they are out of sync with each other, one might be in reverse while the other goes forward, causing an inevitable collision. And if the whistle/horn button is pressed, both engines will sound off at once.

Block systems and command control

Modelers solved this problem by dividing a layout into electrically isolated lengths of track, called *blocks*, each of which is controlled by a toggle switch. A layout may be divided so that different parts of the main line and each siding can be turned on or off, allowing a train on a siding to be unaffected by another train running on the main line. Each block may also have a separate transformer, allowing two or more trains to be operated independently in their own blocks of track.

The block system was the most efficient method for wiring a layout for many decades, until the advent of command control in 1994. Lionel called its system TMCC, or TrainMaster Command Control. In its most basic form, it consists of a rectangular PowerMaster unit wired to the ground circuit of the layout and a handheld

Lionel TMCC and Legacy command control components include a ZW-L Transformer, Legacy Command set, PowerMaster unit, and TMCC remote.

unit with throttle and control buttons for speed, direction, whistle (horn), and a variety of other functions.

This system can be configured to operate most O gauge locomotives, but in order to take advantage of all the TMCC features, such as remote control uncoupling anywhere on the layout, it is necessary to purchase a locomotive equipped with a digital receiver onboard. The major advantage of command control is that two TMCC-equipped locomotives, each with an individual address code, may be operated independently on the same block of track simply by punching a code into the handheld controller.

With command control, it is no longer necessary to divide a layout into individual blocks. Just two wires between the transformer and the track are all that is needed—if all your locomotives contain TMCC electronics.

TrainMaster Command Control was a big step forward in toy train operation, and it has been licensed to both Atlas and Weaver for use in their locomotives. In 2000, MTH (Mike's Train House) Electric Trains introduced DCS (Digital Command System), a competing product that offered advanced features not included in Lionel's product. Lionel countered with its Legacy system in 2006, which is compatible with origi-

nal TMCC locomotives and also has extra features for operating locomotives in the Legacy line.

The MTH and Lionel systems both operate well, and they are proving popular with model railroaders having an interest in digital technology. While TMCC and DCS are not fundamentally compatible, they each have limited ability to operate the other company's equipment.

Both DCS and Legacy offer a host of operating possibilities too extensive to describe here, including impressive onboard sound systems, pinpoint speed control, and remote operation of accessories, all accessed from the handheld unit. It seemed at first that the need for complicated block wiring would soon be as extinct as the dodo bird and that every model railroader might embrace the new technology. But block wiring is still preferred by many toy train enthusiasts who now use digital command control, as well as by those who prefer to run their trains solely with conventional transformers. Operators use conventional wiring for a variety of reasons, including these:

- Command control is expensive, adding from $100–$200 to the price of each locomotive, in addition to the cost of the basic system and its peripheral equipment.

Two or more trains will operate independently on the same track with a command control system, as shown by these trains in Lionel's Legacy line.

- Command control works perfectly when added to a layout that is divided into blocks, so operators can enjoy both methods of operation.
- Advanced features found in modern locomotives, including directional lighting, sophisticated sound systems, and reduced start-up speeds, do not require command control to operate.
- Many toy train enthusiasts, especially those who collect vintage equipment, still enjoy operating their engines with a conventional transformer. To some, the old-fashioned hands-on feel of a ZW throttle handle somehow seems more appropriate when running a prewar *Blue Comet* or a postwar Santa Fe diesel than scrolling through the menus of a handheld controller.

There is evidence that some companies are beginning to recognize that there are still many operators who are not interested in converting to the new technology. For a number of years, Atlas, MTH, and Lionel installed command control technology in most

of their medium-priced and premium locomotives. Only their lower-priced trains, those with lesser cosmetic detail and fewer features, lacked command control electronics.

However, a new trend is appearing. Lionel has begun reissuing updated versions of classic designs from the 1940s and '50s without command control. Perhaps even more significant, Lionel's Signature Edition Catalog features a number of highly detailed scale locomotives, both steam and diesel, which previously would have been offered only with TMCC. But now purchasers have the option of buying these premium engines without TMCC at a lower price. Clearly the company recognizes that there are still many toy train enthusiasts who operate their trains with just a basic transformer.

Another notable trend by Atlas O, Lionel, and MTH is an increasing emphasis upon so-called starter sets, featuring low-priced locomotives with three or four cars prepackaged with a loop of track and a transformer. Such

sets are aimed primarily at the toy market, rather than at serious model railroaders and are designed to attract younger buyers and parents looking for quality toys for their children. As was true decades ago, however, such starter sets can become the genesis for a lifelong interest in model trains and may cultivate the desire to add more equipment for increased fun. If a layout is wired using the methods described in this book, these starter trains will never become outdated and consigned to the shelf.

Therefore, this book is for everyone, no matter how they choose to run their trains. It describes the tried-and-true method of block wiring, which we will call conventional wiring, and which is fully compatible with any three-rail electric trains manufactured in the past hundred years. It is equally compatible with a command control system that can be added at any time without making changes to the basic wiring.

We begin the journey with an overview of basic electricity in Chapter 1.

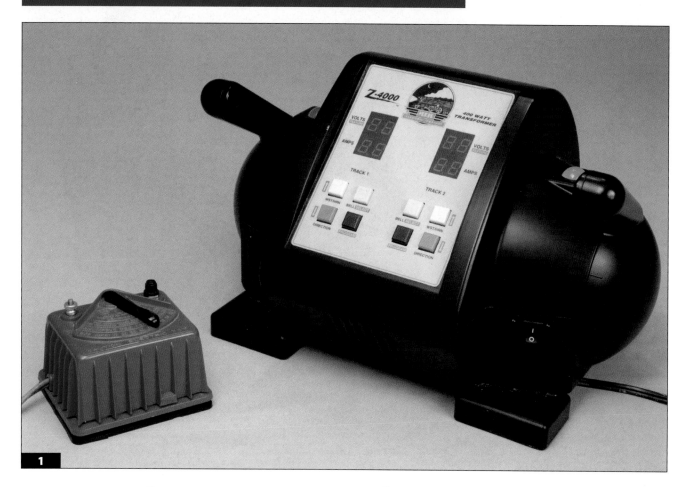

CHAPTER ONE

Understanding electricity

Nothing about electricity should be considered complex or mysterious. It is simply a source of energy, analogous to the water in a fast-flowing river that affects everything in its path while traveling from point A to point B. The energy in a current of water can be used to do some form of work, such as pushing a boat downstream or turning a waterwheel. Just as water flows downhill, propelled by gravity, electrical energy flows from one place to another place. The point of origin is called the *negative pole*, and the point of destination is the *positive pole*. To provide electrical power to operate our trains, we need a transformer that reduces household current to a more usable level, **1.**

The old and the new: a tiny transformer from a decades-old Lionel starter set is dwarfed by a 400-watt powerhouse from MTH. Both transformers provide enough power to run a train.

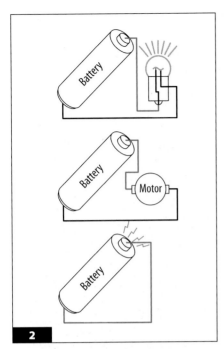

2

A battery can power a lightbulb (top) or a small motor (center). If electricity flows directly between poles, a short circuit occurs (bottom).

3

This is almost certainly the best-known transformer in toy train history—Lionel's ZW model from the postwar years. However complicated a transformer looks on the outside, such as the ZW, it is a simple device on the inside that changes household current from high pressure to low pressure.

Basic circuits

Figure **2** shows a typical battery, in which the flat bottom is the negative pole and the circular protrusion on top is the positive pole. In the top illustration, a bulb has been connected between the poles. The electrical current flows through the internal wiring of the bulb. The S-shaped line in the center of the bulb represents the filament, which is a very thin piece of wire that resists the flow of electricity.

Electrical resistance generates heat, which causes the filament to glow, thus giving off light. This resistance also slows down the transfer of energy between the poles, so that the energy stored in the battery is used more slowly and lasts for a longer period of time. (Electrical resistance is measured in units called *ohms*.)

The energy contained in a battery can also be used to turn a small electric motor, as shown in the center illustration. However, a single battery cannot generate enough energy to run the relatively large motor in a toy locomotive. To do that, you would have to connect several batteries together, as was done in early train sets.

In the bottom illustration, a wire is connected directly between the two poles. This is called a *short circuit* because there is nothing between the negative and positive poles to make use of the energy flow. In this application, the only product of the electrical current is heat, which quickly dissipates the energy stored in the battery.

Amps and volts

The flow of electrical energy is measured by two basic units called *amperage* and *voltage* (or *amps* and *volts*). Amperage is a measure of the volume of electricity available. Using a liquid analogy again, the large volume of water contained in a wide and deep river has the potential to do heavier work than the water in a small stream. A big river can turn a huge waterwheel, while a narrow creek can move only a small one. An electrical current with greater amperage (volume) is similarly capable of a greater amount of work.

Voltage is a measure of the force or pressure of electricity and is essentially independent of amperage. Imagine a broad river that flows across a flat plain with almost no downward slope.

The water will flow slowly. Even though the volume (amperage) of water is large, the lack of force (voltage) behind it moves the water at a leisurely pace. Any waterwheel in its path would turn slowly, if at all.

Now imagine the same volume of water cascading over Niagara Falls. Thanks to gravity, the falling water would exert great force upon a waterwheel in its path and turn it briskly. This is the equivalent of high voltage in an electrical circuit.

Three-rail O gauge trains typically require 2 or more amps of electricity to operate. Small lightweight locomotives with smaller motors need less, while heavy steamers or twin-motor diesels need more. The motors are constructed to operate efficiently between 6–18 volts. At low voltage (low pressure or force), a motor will run slowly, while more volts produces increased speed.

In the absence of sufficient amperage, however, no amount of voltage will cause a large motor to turn. The force may be present, but without sufficient volume to back it up, nothing happens. Similarly, high amperage alone will not run a motor without enough voltage to propel the current forward.

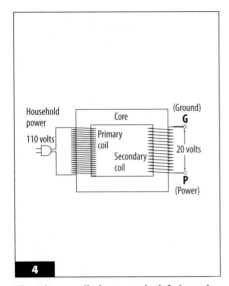

4 The primary coil, shown on the left, is made up of many turns of small diameter wire, and the secondary coil (on the right) has fewer turns of thicker wire.

5 This interior view of a vintage Lionel ZW Transformer shows a secondary coil at the top and two rheostat rollers, one of which (left) is for one of the two throttles and the other is for one of the two variable voltage circuits. The other two rollers (not visible) are on the opposite side of the secondary coil.

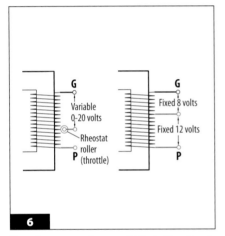

6 Transformers can have variable (left) or fixed (right) voltage posts for operating accessories.

7 Efficient, modern transformers, clockwise from upper left, include the MTH Z-4000, Lionel ZW with separate power supply, and Atlas O's 80-watt transformer featured in its starter sets.

For example, consider the small, rectangular 9-volt battery that is used in smoke alarms and a variety of portable devices. Since a toy train's motor will operate on 9 volts, you might think such a battery would do the job, but the volume of energy contained in a battery is relative to its size. The energy available in a small 9-volt battery is only a small fraction of 1 amp. Just as a trickle of water is insufficient to move a big waterwheel, no matter how fast it is moving, a small battery cannot move a large toy train motor, even though enough pressure (voltage) is available.

In order to run our trains, we need a supply of electricity with both sufficient volume (amps) and force (volts),

and the supply of current must be consistent. The most efficient way to obtain this power is from a household electrical supply. The average modern home is supplied with a total of 200 amps, with 15 or more amps available at each wall plug, which is more than adequate for even very large train layouts. However, the level of voltage is approximately 110–115, far too high for our 6- to 20-volt locomotive motors. That is why we need a transformer.

Transformers

A toy train transformer is a relatively simple device that changes household current from high pressure to low pressure (high voltage to low voltage), **3**.

It contains a metallic core wrapped with two coils of wire, **4**. The primary coil is made up of many turns of small diameter wire, and the secondary coil has fewer turns of thicker wire. The two coils do not touch each other. The primary coil is connected to the household current, and the secondary coil connects to the train track.

When a 110-volt household current passes through the primary coil, it produces a powerful magnetic field. By a process called *induction*, this generates a weaker magnetic field in the secondary coil, resulting in lower voltage. The amount of voltage reduction is a function of the size and number of turns of the wire in the two coils. A toy

The power posts on this modern transformer are clearly identifiable by their red color.

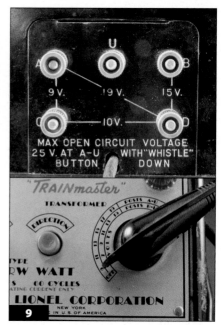

On the back of this Lionel RW Transformer (top), the letter U designates the throttle. On the top of the transformer, the label on the throttle dial shows the voltage available with posts AU and BU.

train transformer reduces the 110-volt household current to a much more useful and safer maximum of 18–20 volts.

There is a fundamental difference between the electricity produced by a battery and that which is available in our homes, although for practical purposes it has no effect on how we think about the way our trains operate. A battery produces *direct current* (DC), in which the flow of energy always travels in one direction, from the negative pole to the positive pole. Household power is *alternating current* (AC), which in North America reverses direction 60 times each second. It is easier to understand the diagrams in this book if we continue to think of the current as flowing in one direction from one pole to the other. We call the source pole Power and the destination pole Ground (labeled P and G in the figures).

The 20 volts generated by the secondary coil of a transformer causes a toy train motor to run very fast. In order to control the speed of a train, we need a means for varying the amount of voltage that reaches the track. Virtually all transformers made from the late 1930s until today's electronic units achieved this speed control through a device called a *rheostat*.

The speed control handle of a transformer (the throttle) is attached to a metal roller or flat wiper that moves back and forth across the secondary coil, **5**. Depending upon where it contacts the coil, it taps a greater or lesser amount of voltage to control the speed of the train, which is called *variable voltage*. (Modern transformers achieve

the same sort of variable voltage control electronically rather than mechanically, but the end result is the same.)

Small transformers, such as the one in photo **1**, have only two posts to which wires may be connected. One post is the ground connection, wired to one end of the secondary coil, and the other post is connected to the rheostat roller. The voltage produced is lower when the roller is near the ground connection and higher when it moves away from the ground. Some large transformers have two rheostats and two throttle handles, and they can run two trains simultaneously at different speeds in separate blocks of track.

Larger transformers also have additional posts for connecting wires to operate accessories. These posts are usually wired to fixed points on the secondary coil to provide various levels of fixed voltage, **6**. On the right side of the figure, you'll see two such fixed voltage ranges: the 12-volt circuit is suitable for some types of accessories, and the 8-volt circuit is good for lighting lampposts and buildings. The combination of these two voltages (8 + 12) equals the overall capacity of the secondary coil (20 volts).

Some transformers, such as those in Atlas train sets and Lionel's ZW, also have variable voltage posts for accessories. The voltage is adjusted by control dials or levers mounted on the cases.

Watts and volt-amps

The capacity of a transformer to perform work is commonly measured in units called *watts* (named after James

Watt, who developed the reciprocating steam engine near the end of the 18th century and made railroading possible). In general, watts are a measure of the reserve amount of power available from a particular device, such as a stereo amplifier, a microwave oven, or a toy train transformer.

To understand how a watt functions, imagine turning on a water faucet in the sink. If the handle is turned on all the way, a substantial stream gushes out. Then, turn on all the faucets in the house, and you will find the flow of water at each location is reduced.

A small transformer with small internal coils produces relatively modest wattage—enough to operate one locomotive, a few lights, and one or two accessories, but that's all. If you overload it with too much equipment, it's like turning on too many faucets at once. There isn't enough power to go around, and everything slows down. This is an inherently unsafe condition called an *overload*.

The transformers that come with inexpensive train and trolley sets may produce as little as 20–40 watts. They can run the equipment they come with, but they allow little opportunity

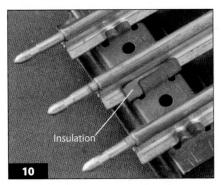

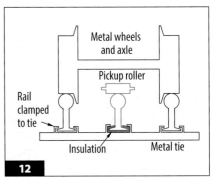

10 On this 50-year-old section of Lionel O gauge track, the middle rail is also clamped to the ties but is separated from them by pieces of thin fiber insulation.

11 Lionel lockons make wiring attachments easy, but they don't resemble anything found on a real railroad.

12 Resting on the outer rails, the metal wheels are in contact with the ground side of a circuit. The middle rail is insulated.

for expansion. Larger starter sets have 80- to 100-watt transformers, which have more reserve power for extra accessories. For running multiple trains and powering layouts with many lights and accessories, you will need high-output transformers with bigger coils. The largest transformers on today's market produce between 400 watts of power (MTH Z-4000) and as much as 720 watts (Lionel ZW).

Using current terminology, the power reserve of most transformers, such as those sold by Lionel and MTH, is rated in watts. Atlas refers to an 80-watt capacity when describing its transformer in the company's Industrial Rail starter sets. However, on the unit's metal identification plate, the capacity is stated in volt-amps (VA). For all practical purposes, 1 watt equals 1 volt-amp. Mathematically, a single watt is any ratio of amps times volts that equals 1. For example, a power source that produces 6 volts at .1666 amps equals 1 watt. In the case of a transformer, the terms watts and volt-amps are interchangeable—an 80-watt transformer is also an 80 VA transformer. (A distinction is made between the two terms when applied to computer equipment, but that is of no consequence to the circuits described in this book.)

Choosing a transformer

Lionel and other manufacturers such as American Flyer and Marx sold vast numbers of transformers of all sizes during the two decades following World War II. They are amazingly durable,

and many model railroaders (including myself) still use them. However, if you are just starting out in the hobby, I do not recommend them for the following reasons:

- While there is little that can go wrong with a transformer's main circuit, the internal wiring can deteriorate over time and create a safety hazard. Other internal components may need servicing or replacement, such as the rheostat roller or wiper and the circuit used to blow whistles and horns. Such repairs require specialized knowledge and should be entrusted only to experienced personnel.
- Older transformers are less safe than their modern counterparts. Many lack an on/off switch and must be unplugged after use, which is easy to forget, especially by children.
- Circuit breakers in vintage transformers are slow to react to an overload or short circuit, which is another safety concern. Some models lack a circuit breaker entirely and are prone to overheating if overloaded. Modern transformers react almost instantaneously to an overload, which is a major safety advantage. Equally important, an overload or a short circuit may damage the electronic circuits in modern locomotives and accessories if the circuit breaker is slow to react.
- Older transformers are inefficient and deliver somewhat less than their rated power capacity. A modern 100-watt transformer has significantly greater capacity than a 100-watt unit from the 1950s.

- The majority of older transformers have a whistle/horn button, but they lack a second one to operate the bells and other sound features in some modern locomotives. A separate bell button is also required to operate the remote control couplers and other functions on MTH Protosound locomotives.

Three manufacturers of train sets offer safe and efficient transformers in various price ranges for any size train layout, **7**. Even those transformers packaged with starter sets can provide advanced features. Atlas packs an 80-watt unit with its starter sets as well as in some sets sold by Williams by Bachmann. In addition to the throttle, this transformer has a separate variable voltage circuit for accessories and buttons for direction, whistle/ horn, and bell. The variable voltage circuit is an especially valuable feature, as it allows you to control the speed of the motors in some accessories. The transformer's capacity is sufficient for any medium-size layout with one large or two small locomotives and a variety of accessories.

In addition to a compact 100-watt transformer, MTH makes a 400-watt unit (Z-4000) that has two separate throttles and two fixed voltage posts, plus duplicate bell and whistle/horn controls. The Z-4000 has an internal power supply with amp and volt meters for each of the two throttles and a programming button for use with the DCS command control system.

Lionel sells an 80-watt model and also a modern version of its famous

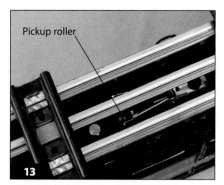

13

Pickup rollers gather current from the middle rail, while the wheels are grounded to the outside rails.

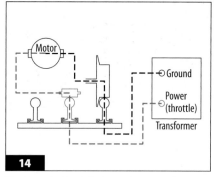

14

The throttle circuit is shown in red and the ground side of a circuit in black.

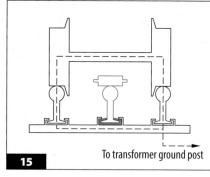

15

To transformer ground post

Both outer rails are grounded to the transformer.

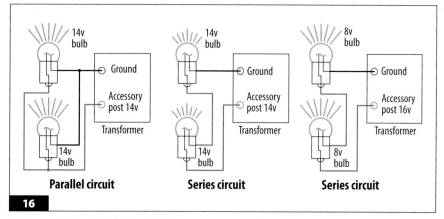

16

Parallel circuit   Series circuit   Series circuit

In this parallel circuit (left), both bulbs receive 14 volts of power. In the series circuit (center), each bulb receives 7 volts, and in the series circuit at right, each bulb receives 8 volts.

ZW, which first appeared on the market in 1948. The main body of the new ZW looks very much like the original version, but it does not contain a built-in power supply. Instead, one to four external power supplies must be plugged into the main unit. Each power supply is rated at 180 watts, allowing an operator to configure the transformer to 180, 360, 540 or 720 watts, according to the size of a layout and its power requirements. The ZW has two separate throttles and two variable voltage controls. The newer ZW-L, with a 720-watt built-in power supply, features refined speed control and has meters that monitor electrical output.

Vintage Lionel transformers

When wiring transformers, the ground and power posts on modern transformers are clearly identified, **8**. For example, on the MTH Z-4000, power posts are red and ground posts are black. On a Lionel ZW, everything is identified in large white letters. Today, the universal label for the ground post is the letter U.

However, not all vintage Lionel transformers labeled the ground this way, and on some models, such as the popular 1033 transformer included in many thousands of postwar O-27 train sets, the letter U designates the throttle.

Also, some transformers have two variable voltage ranges connected to the same throttle, **9**. These two ranges are obtained by using different ground posts and were provided to accommodate both large and small locomotive motors found in toy trains. Typically, larger, more expensive trains require higher

voltage, while lightweight and inexpensive locomotives draw less current. The two voltage ranges provide the correct amount of current for each type.

Because of the number of vintage Lionel transformers still in use, I have provided the chart on page 13. It lists most Lionel transformer models made between 1939 and 1969 and shows the ground and variable voltage (throttle) posts and the amount of voltage they provide. The number of throttles is indicated by the number in parentheses after the model number. Fixed voltage posts are also given when used in conjunction with the ground post or posts.

Power to the train

In order for the motor in a locomotive to run, it must receive a dependable supply of power from the transformer, but because the train must be free to move, you cannot connect wires directly to the engine. Instead you need to wire the transformer to the track. O gauge trains run on three-rail track,

in which the two outer rails (those supporting the train's wheels) are connected to the ground side of the transformer's power circuit. The middle rail is connected to the power side of the circuit (the throttle handle), **10**.

Lionel first began making three-rail O gauge track in 1915 and continues to sell a virtually identical product today. Because all of the parts of the track are metal, the ties and the two outer rails are interconnected electrically. The middle rail, however, is isolated from the ties and outer rails by fiber insulating strips.

Many years ago, Lionel engineers created a simple device for attaching wires to a layout. They called it a *lockon* after the manner in which it fastens to the track, **11**. It consists of a non-metallic rectangle, two devices called Fahnestock clips to which wires may be attached, and thin metal bars that attach the lockon firmly to the middle rail and one outside rail. The clips are numbered 1 and 2. A wire from the throttle post of the transformer is attached to clip 1 and therefore to the middle rail, and the ground wire connects to clip 2 and an outside rail.

The metal wheels of a locomotive conduct electricity through the frame to the motor. On the underside of a locomotive, two or more metal rollers are positioned between the wheels. These rollers are insulated from the wheels and the frame. When a locomotive is placed on the track, the metal wheels rest on the outer rails and are in contact with the ground side of the circuit, **12**.

The rollers ride on the middle rail to receive power from the throttle side of the circuit, **13**. These rollers are usually referred to as *pickup rollers* because they pick up current from the middle rail. Figure **14** shows the route that electricity takes between the transformer and the locomotive motor. It is common practice for the ground side of a circuit to be shown in black on wiring diagrams, and for the power (throttle) side of the circuit to be shown in color. (With a few exceptions, this convention is generally followed throughout the book.)

Because the two outer rails of the track are clamped directly to the metal ties, both rails are grounded to the transformer, **15**. In recent years, there have been many new styles of O gauge track introduced by various manufacturers, all of which are much more realistic than the traditional design. In some of these products, the two outside rails are connected together, while in others, they are electrically independent. In general, there is no significant difference in the way the trains operate because the wheels of the train transfer the ground from one rail to the other. However, the independent rails allow us to connect certain types of accessories such as trackside signals quickly and easily. (These new track products are described in Chapters 3, 4, and 10.)

Series and parallel circuits

To this point, we have discussed only simple circuits, in which an electrical device is operated by two wires (power

Lionel transformer voltage posts

Model	Ground	Variable voltage	Fixed voltage
1032, 1033, 1044 (1)	A	U (5-16 volts)	B (5 volts)
	A	—	C (16 volts)
	B	U (0-11 volts)	C (11 volts)
1034 (1)	A	U (10-20 volts)	B (6 volts)
	A	—	C (20 volts)
	B	U (4-14 volts)	A (6 volts)
	B	—	C (14 volts)
1144 (1)	A	U (10-20 volts)	B (6 volts)
	A	—	C (20 volts)
	B	U (6-16 volts)	A (6 volts)
	B	—	C (14 volts)
A, Q (1)	A	U (14-24 volts)	B (8 volts)
	A	—	C (14 volts)
	B	U (6-16 volts)	A (8 volts)
	B	—	C (6 volts)
KW (2)	U	A (6-20 volts)	C (6 volts)
	U	B (6-20 volts)	D (20 volts)
	C	A (0-14 volts)	D (14 volts)
	C	B (0-14 volts)	U (6 volts)
LW (1)	A	U (6-20 volts)	B (16 volts)
	A		C (14 volts)
R (2)	A	C (14-24 volts)	B (8 volts)
	A	F (14-24 volts)	D (14 volts)
	B	C (6-16 volts)	A (8 volts)
	B	F (6-16 volts)	E (16 volts)
	D	—	E (10 volts)
RW (1)	A	U (10-19 volts)	C (9 volts)
	A	—	D (19 volts)
	B	U (6-16 volts)	C (6 volts)
	B	—	D (16 volts)
	D	—	C (10 volts)
S (1)	A	U (10-19 volts)	B (5 volts)
	A	—	C (19 volts)
	B	U (5-14 volts)	C (14 volts)
SW (2)	U	A (7-18 volts)	B (18 volts)
	U	D (7-18 volts)	C (14 volts)
TW (1)	A	U (7-18 volts)	C (18 volts)
	A	—	D (14 volts)
	B	U (0-11 volts)	A (7 volts)
	E	—	F (14 volts)
V, Z (2+2)*	U	A (6-24 volts)	—
	U	B (6-24 volts)	—
	U	C (6-24 volts)	—
	U	D (6-24 volts)	—
VW, ZW (2+2)*	U	A (6-20 volts)	—
	U	B (6-20 volts)	—
	U	C (6-20 volts)	—
	U	D (6-20 volts)	—

*All posts on these transformers offer variable voltage. A and D are designated as throttles and are equipped with direction and whistle controls. B and C are to be set by the operator to preferred voltages (such as 10 and 14) and left there, but they could be used as throttles if connected to the track. However, B and C do not have direction and whistle controls.

17

Flat-bladed (left) and Phillips-head screwdrivers (right) come in many sizes. The large screwdriver in the center has interchangeable ends of various sizes and types.

18

A variety of miniature screwdrivers are needed when working with today's sophisticated O gauge trains and accessories. They can be purchased economically in sets such as this one.

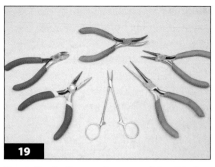

19

Specialized pliers perform a variety of tasks. In the center is a medical hemostat, useful for holding small parts securely. The pliers with the blue grips (top left) is a cutting tool that can be used to strip wires.

and ground) coming from a transformer. If a miniature lightbulb rated at 14 volts is connected to a transformer circuit providing 14 volts, it will glow brightly. Lower the voltage to 12, and the bulb will be somewhat dimmer but last longer before burning out. Increase the voltage to 16 or 18, and the bulb will become very bright, but its life span will be shortened.

Two or more 14-volt bulbs may be powered by a single 14-volt circuit. In a parallel circuit, shown at left in figure **16**, two bulbs are each connected to both the power and ground posts of the transformer, and both receive a full 14 volts of power.

In a series circuit, as in the middle diagram in figure **16**, the power from the transformer passes into the lower bulb and then through it directly to the second bulb before the connection to the ground post. As a result, each bulb receives half the current, 7 volts, and glows much less brightly. A series circuit is often used where you want the bulbs to have a very long life or in model railroad buildings where a soft glow is considered to be most realistic. In the right-hand drawing of figure **16**, two 8-volt bulbs are wired in series into a 16-volt circuit. Each bulb receives 8 volts, half of the circuit's capacity, and glows brightly. If these bulbs were wired in parallel, each would receive a full 16 volts, be extremely bright, and would burn out very quickly.

If you replace the bulbs in these circuits with two 14-volt motors, such as those found in accessories, exactly

the same conditions would apply. In a parallel circuit, the motors would each receive a full 14 volts and run rapidly. In a series circuit, each motor would receive half the voltage and run slowly. In general, however, accessories are almost never wired in series because they are normally operated one at a time, and most operate best at 12–14 volts. (Applications of series and parallel circuits appear in subsequent chapters.)

Tools and hardware

To complete most of the wiring on a train layout, you will need a basic set of tools and a supply of electrical hardware. Many of them you may already own, and most are available from hardware stores and automobile or electronics supply stores. Tools can be a lifetime investment. Some of the ones pictured in this chapter are more than 80 years old, passed down to me from my father, and have helped to build more than two dozen layouts. While they may look a bit worn, they still do the job.

Screwdrivers. Because toy train components are assembled with many different sizes and types of screws, you will need a variety of standard-size screwdrivers with Phillips heads as well as flat blades for slotted screws, **17**. In general, modern trains have mostly Phillips head screws, while prewar and postwar trains have mainly slotted head screws. Miniature screwdrivers with flat blades and Phillips heads are handy for the tiny screws used in accessories such as turnout controllers and circuit boards, **18**.

Pliers. Like miniature screwdrivers, smaller pliers intended for electrical work also come in economical sets or can be purchased individually, **19**. Needle-nose pliers have long tapered ends for reaching into tight places, and others have blades for cutting wires. A special gripping tool is a hemostat, which has a locking mechanism on the handle that holds the jaws closed. This medical clamp is also a valuable tool for model railroaders. It serves as a third hand to keep wires and small parts in place during soldering and other chores.

Wire stripper. You can strip insulation from the end of a wire with cutting pliers, but a wire stripper will do the job much more neatly and efficiently, **20**. Two types are commonly available. A handheld model has a series of small, rounded cutting blades near the center of the tool that are sized for various thicknesses of wire. It also has jaws for crimping lugs onto the ends of wires and straight blades at the end for cutting. This tool is relatively easy to use, but it can be a bit hard on the hands if you have a lot of wires to strip.

The semiautomatic type is a single-purpose tool that lacks the crimping and cutting features of the handheld model, but it removes insulation much more easily and precisely. The spring-loaded jaws hold the wire securely, and a light squeeze on the handle exposes the end of the wire quickly and neatly. (It's more expensive, but definitely easier on the hands.)

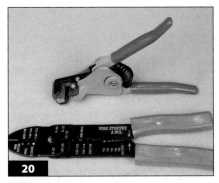

20

Semiautomatic (top) and handheld (bottom) wire strippers expose the ends of wires more precisely than pliers with cutting blades.

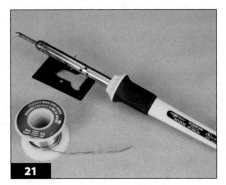

21

A 30-watt iron is adequate for most soldering tasks on a model railroad.

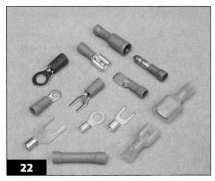

22

Electrical connectors make connecting wires simple. They feature a variety of tips and are usually connected to wire ends simply by being crimped with pliers.

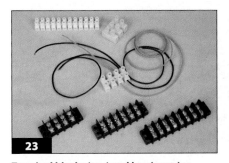

23

Terminal blocks (top) and barrier strips help keep wiring neat and secure, which is essential on a layout. You will want to trace wiring connections easily when repairs and maintenance are necessary.

24

Toggle switches (left) and slide switches (right) are two types of switches that you may want to use for operating accessories on your toy train layout.

25

Electronic relays often come with convenient plug-in bases that provide screws for connecting wires.

Soldering iron and solder. Most wiring jobs can be accomplished with electrical connectors, but there are instances where you will have to solder wires to miniature toggle switches and for some other connections. A 30- or 35-watt model is best for electronic applications, **21**. Use only rosin-core solder for wiring—avoid acid-core solder, which is meant for joining metal parts together. (See page 91 for a description of soldering techniques.)

Electrical connectors. Various kinds of electrical connectors make wiring jobs neat and easy, **22**. They are available in many shapes and sizes from electronics supply stores. You will find several different types described in the following chapters in situations where their use is most appropriate.

Barrier strips and terminal blocks. Barrier strips and terminal blocks help keep your wiring organized, **23**. A barrier strip consists of 4, 6, or 8

pairs of screws mounted on nonconducting material, such as plastic. The two screws of each pair are connected together electrically by a metal strip, but there is no connection between adjacent pairs. The term *barrier strip* is suggested by the narrow raised fences between pairs of screws that prevent wires from touching nearby screws. (Also see Chapter 4.)

A terminal block is made from plastic and contains small metal tubes into which wires may be inserted. These blocks come in strips of 8, 10, or 12 and may be cut apart with a razor saw. They also come in various sizes to accommodate both small and large gauge wires. Miniature machine screws are fitted into the tops of the blocks and extend downward into the tubes. Tightening the screws holds the wires securely inside. Terminal blocks with large openings allow you to connect two or more wires together on the same side (see Chapter 4).

Switches and relays. Switches are electrical devices for turning current on or off and are an essential hardware item for any model railroad, **24**. Simple on/off or push-button switches come packaged with most accessories, but you may wish to use other types, such as slide switches, on your control panel, as described in Chapter 4. (The term *switch* can also refer to a section of track with moveable rails. To avoid any confusion, we will use *switch* throughout the book only to describe the electrical type, and track switches will be referred to as *turnouts*.)

A relay is an electrical switch that is used to throw other switches, **25**. It provides a highly reliable means for controlling different types of automatic accessories, especially those that respond to a passing train. For threerail O gauge trains, choose the 12-volt AC variety (see Chapter 8).

To begin our study of train layout wiring, we will open up and assemble a typical starter set in Chapter 2.

CHAPTER TWO

1

Wiring a simple layout

Today's inexpensive starter sets, such as this Atlas Industrial Rail product, feature sturdy, attractive, and dependable locomotives and cars.

It is almost certain that most serious model railroaders who grew up during the 1940s and '50s first became interested in the hobby through playing with a Lionel, American Flyer, or Marx train set. These popular toys were high on many girls' and boys' Christmas lists. During subsequent decades, children's interest in trains waned somewhat, replaced by fascination with slot cars, space-related toys (following the launch of Russia's Sputnik satellite in 1957), and later the first primitive but enthralling video games such as Pong.

Opening a train set box for the first time is an exciting adventure for children.

For a number of years thereafter, model railroading became mainly the province of middle-aged and older enthusiasts, a trend that did not bode well for the long-term survival of the hobby. During the 1970s, '80s, and '90s, Lionel continued to market basic train sets, but with nowhere near the success of the immediate postwar period. When Mike Wolf began marketing O gauge electric trains under his own brand name (Mike's Train House, later MTH) in 1993, he targeted the adult market. Much of his company's efforts centered around the sale of separate locomotives and rolling stock, many of which were built to accurate scale and highly detailed. Economical starter sets were not included in early production.

To meet the MTH competition, Lionel also began to emphasize higher end products, a trend that continues today. Each year MTH and Lionel, along with Atlas O, 3rd Rail, and Weaver, produce an ever-growing variety of beautiful locomotives and rolling stock that rivals the real thing

in appearance and operation. All of this excellence comes at a high price, however. Locomotives in the $1,000–$2,000 range are becoming more common.

Starter sets

Recently, however, such organizations as the Train Collectors Association (TCA) and the manufacturers themselves have mounted a serious effort to introduce more young people to the pleasures of collecting and operating toy trains. The TCA has formed a kids club to encourage parents to interest their children in the hobby. With a number of products being produced by Atlas, Lionel, and MTH, there is strong evidence for a resurgence in the popularity of the traditional train set, prepackaged to include everything needed to set up and operate a rudimentary miniature railroad, **1**.

The Atlas Industrial Rail set pictured in photo **2** is typical of current offerings by the major manufacturers. This set consists of a well-proportioned

Atlantic-type steam locomotive and tender, two passenger cars (a combine and a coach), a loop of sectional track with integrated roadbed, a transformer, hookup wires, a tube of smoke fluid, and a detailed instruction booklet. Similar sets with freight cars instead of coaches and a Christmas theme are also available. Each locomotive is equipped with remote control reverse, a whistle, a bell, and a smoke generator.

Atlas O Industrial Rail track

Industrial Rail track represents a major improvement in realistic appearance over the common three-tie sections. The shape of the rails is similar to the real thing, and they are held in place by simulated spikes molded into dark brown plastic ties. Light tan simulated stone ballast provides an attractive contrast to the ties. There are 12 sections of curved track and 6 sections of straight track. Lionel and MTH both manufacture similar products, and Atlas supplies its track for sets sold by Williams by Bachmann.

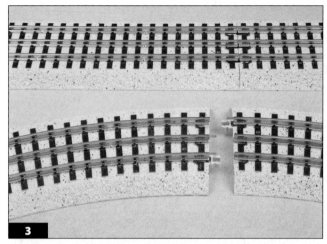

3

Today's starter sets feature realistic track with integrated roadbed. The sections snap together securely, and flat pins in the ends of the rails assure good electrical contact.

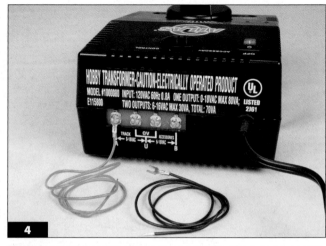

4

This Atlas starter-set transformer is easy to wire. The red wire goes to post A and the black wire to either of the U (ground) posts. It features a separate circuit for accessories (post B). Connections to the posts are easily made with the spade lugs on the end of the wires.

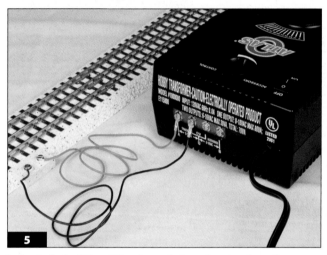

5

Instead of a traditional Lionel-type lockon, the wires from the transformer are screwed to a special terminal section of Atlas track.

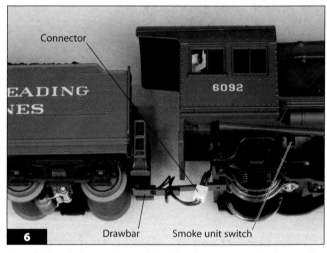

6

A small electrical connector and two drawbars connect the locomotive with the tender. Note the smoke unit switch under the cab.

The Atlas trains themselves are relatively small, falling somewhere between O scale and S scale in size, and this has several advantages in a starter set. The equipment is relatively light in weight and is sized properly for children's small hands. However, while these sets are meant to be attractive to children, the realism of the locomotive and coaches also appeals to adults who are just beginning to investigate the hobby. Full-scale coaches would overwhelm the small radius track that comes with most starter sets, but the scaled-down Atlas cars are well proportioned and look very realistic—long and graceful instead of stubby, foreshortened, and toy-like.

The train set is very easy to set up, following the concise instructions contained in the instruction manual. The ends of each track section have molded plastic tabs that snap securely into slots on adjoining sections, **3**. Small flat metal pins in the ends of the T-shaped rails provide electrical continuity from section to section. Children will probably need supervision when assembling the track for the first time to be sure that the pins line up correctly, but they should be able to master the technique quickly.

There are four wire connection points on the back of the transformer, clearly labeled as to their purpose, **4**. Post A is the power (throttle) post, post B is for accessories, and there are

two ground posts (labeled U, the common designation for ground), which are connected together internally. To run the trains, you must attach the red wire to post A and the black wire to one of the ground posts. It really doesn't matter which ground post you choose, although using the one closest to post A makes the most sense, as it keeps the track power connections close together. Each wire comes with a small U-shaped spade lug attached, making connections simple. Just loosen the screw on the transformer post, slide the open end of the lug under the top of the screw, and screw it down tight.

One of the straight track sections, called a *terminal section*, is equipped with two screw posts, **5**. The screw on

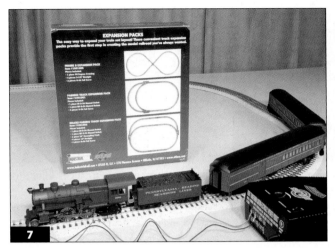

7

The train can be ready to run in less than 30 minutes. Lay out the track, hook up the transformer, connect the locomotive and cars, and place the train on the track.

8

To eliminate this short circuit, move the wheels away from the middle rail and back onto the outside rails.

9

On a vintage transformer, a red overload light warns of a short circuit or an overload caused by having too many trains and accessories connected to the transformer.

10

A small nail or stray piece of metal lodged between the rails can cause a short circuit.

11

When attaching wires to a lockon, keep the stripped ends short to avoid their touching each other and causing a short circuit.

the right connects to the middle rail under the roadbed, while the screw on the left connects to both of the outside rails. Attach the red wire to the right-hand screw and the black wire to the left-hand screw. The throttle power now goes to the middle rail, and the outside rails are grounded.

If the wires are reversed, the train will still operate. However, if you connect them that way, with the throttle post wired to the outside rails and the ground post connected to the middle rail, the whistle button will ring the bell, and the bell button will blow the whistle. If you expand the layout at a later date to include such accessories as the Atlas 21st Century Signal (shown in photo **1**), you will encounter wiring problems. Other difficulties will also arise as the layout is expanded. Therefore, always connect a transformer's throttle post to the middle rail and the ground post (U) to the outside rails.

To prepare the locomotive to run, you must first remove a plug from the smokestack. Then locate the two halves of a tiny electrical connector which are attached to wires leading from the tender and from the locomotive and join them together, **6**. There is only one way to connect them correctly, so don't force them if they don't seem to want to slide into one another. Just turn one half of the connector over and try again. Then insert the drawbar of the locomotive into the slot in the drawbar of the tender and place the locomotive and tender on the track.

If you wish to have the locomotive produce smoke, add 4–6 drops of smoke fluid to the stack. Otherwise, turn off the smoke unit with the switch located under the right side of the cab. The train should never be run with the smoke unit turned on if there is no fluid in the stack, as the unit may overheat and burn out.

Place the coaches on the track and couple them to each other and to the tender, **7**. The train is now ready to run. Turn on the transformer and slowly turn the throttle dial clockwise until the train begins to move forward. If you press the direction button, the locomotive will stop and remain in neutral when you release the button. Press the button again and the train will go into reverse. Repeat the cycle to move forward again. (This reversing sequence was introduced by the Ives Corporation in the mid-1920s, and has been standard in the industry ever since.)

To blow the whistle, press the whistle button firmly. To sound the bell, press the bell button. You don't have to hold the bell button down. It will continue to ring until you press the button again.

If the train does not move when you advance the throttle, the most probable cause is that one or more of the

A loose or broken piece of insulation can allow the middle rail to touch the tie and cause a short circuit.

A loose wire on a transformer post is one of the most common causes of an open circuit. Check to make sure the screws on the posts are tight.

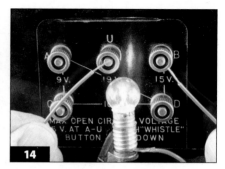

You can look for an open circuit by using a test light made from a 14-volt bulb, a socket, and two wires. Touch the wires to the ground and power posts of the transformer, and the bulb should light.

Use the test light to check the other end of the circuit. If it lights, the problem is probably within the locomotive or accessory, and if it doesn't light, the problem is somewhere between the transformer and the track or accessory.

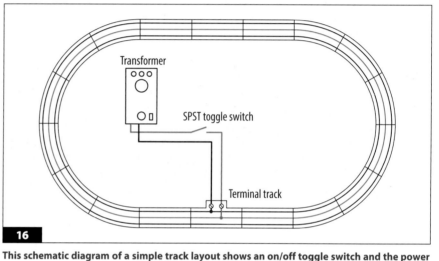

This schematic diagram of a simple track layout shows an on/off toggle switch and the power and ground wires from the transformer connected to a terminal track.

wheels are not on the track. This will usually cause a short circuit, which trips the circuit breaker, lighting the overload lamp on the transformer, and interrupts power to the track. Turn off the transformer and turn the throttle completely counter-clockwise. Make sure all wheels are on the track. When you turn the transformer back on, the circuit breaker resets.

Short circuits

A short circuit (or *short*) is simply the result of current going where it shouldn't. If both the ground and power connections are connected correctly and kept separate from one another, the trains will run. A short occurs whenever there is a direct connection between the power and ground sides of a circuit, such as when the wheels of a train derail and come in contact with the middle rail, **8**. A short

circuit diverts the current from the lights and motors and other devices on the layout and causes them to stop working.

On a modern transformer, a short will cause a built-in circuit breaker to open, which cuts off all current. On some transformers, you will hear a clicking sound when the breaker opens. There is a reset button to restore the flow of current, but it will not work until the cause of the short is corrected.

Vintage transformers may not have a circuit breaker or may have one that is not very efficient. Signs of a short circuit include sparks at the site of the short, a humming or snapping sound, or a dimming of the layout lights. Many older transformers, except very small or early units, have a red overload light that comes on when a short circuit occurs, **9**. This

light may also come on if too many trains and accessories are connected to a transformer without sufficient capacity to run them. A short circuit or overload condition causes a vintage transformer to overheat, a dangerous condition under most circumstances. Vintage transformers usually do not have reset buttons. An open circuit breaker will reset itself when the transformer cools, usually within a minute, but only if the short has been eliminated.

One hard-to-locate short circuit occurs when a stray piece of metal, such as a nail or small screw, becomes lodged between the rails somewhere on the layout, **10**. To find the short if the layout is divided into blocks, first turn them all off and then turn the transformer on. Turn on each block one at a time. When the circuit breaker opens (or the overload light comes on),

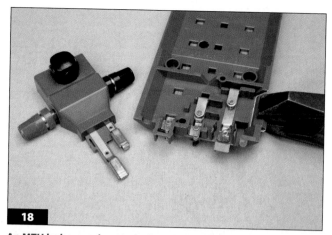

18

An MTH lockon can be attached to any section of track by snapping out a rectangle of plastic in the base with pliers.

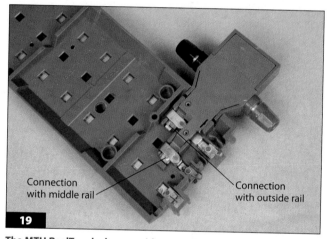

Connection with middle rail

Connection with outside rail

19

The MTH RealTrax lockon provides a power connection to the middle rail and a ground connection to one outside rail.

17

MTH RealTrax sections are substantially built and snap together firmly. When snapped together, the metal fingers press at the ends against each other (center). With the track turned over (top), all of the electrical connections are completely hidden.

you have located the block in which the short may be found. This will limit the area you have to search in order to remedy the problem.

Another common place for a short to occur is at a traditional lockon or underneath an accessory, where the end of a wire attached to one Fahnestock clip touches the other, **11**. Sometimes a wire will work itself loose from a transformer post and touch another post. These conditions are often the result of vibration from passing trains. To avoid this problem, keep the wires as short as possible.

One of the hardest shorts to locate is a loose or broken piece of insulation between the middle rail and a tie on a traditional track section, **12**. Unless the fault is easily visible, to locate the offending piece of track, you may have to disconnect one section at a time. To solve, either repair the insulation or replace the track section.

Open circuits

The opposite of a short circuit is an *open circuit*, a condition whereby no current flows anywhere. The two most common causes are an open circuit breaker or a loose wire. If nothing on the layout works, push the reset button on the circuit breaker first. If there is still no power, look for a loose wire on a transformer post, **13**. If the problem exists in a limited area—a single block of track or when operating a particular accessory—trace the various wires going to that location until you find one that has come loose from a Fahnestock clip, terminal block, or barrier strip. If you have labeled all the wires coming from your control panel, this task is made easier (see Chapter 6).

If you can't find a loose wire, make a simple test light from a 14-volt bulb, a socket, and two wires, **14**. Start by

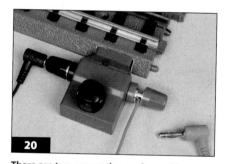

20

There are two connection options with an MTH lockon. At left, the black (ground) wire is shown connected using a convenient plug. At right, the red (power) wire has been inserted through a hole in the shaft that accepts the end of a wire.

touching the wires to the ground and power posts of the transformer. The bulb should light. If not, be sure the circuit breaker has been reset. Because toy train transformers are very reliable and long-lived, it is highly unlikely—although not impossible—that the

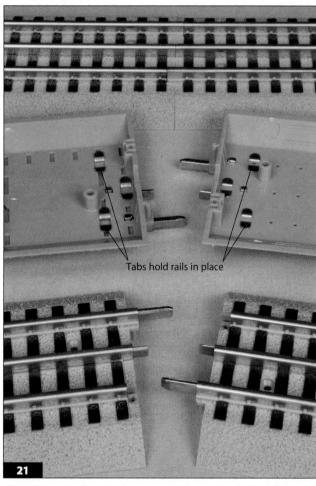

Tabs hold rails in place

The rails on Lionel FasTrack are arranged asymmetrically. When two sections are joined, the short pins in the middle rails slide in next to each other for a secure electrical connection.

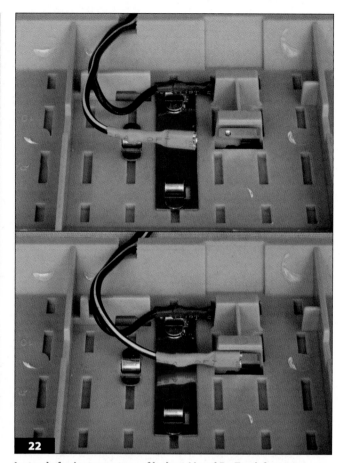

22

Instead of using some type of lockon, Lionel FasTrack features hidden wiring beneath the roadbed. In the top photo, a ground wire (black) is already connected to a plate attached to an outside rail, while the power wire (red) is about to be connected. In the bottom photo, the power wire has been attached.

problem is internal. If that is the case, refer the unit to a qualified repair facility.

Next, use the test light to check the opposite end of the circuit, such as the point where it connects to the track or accessory, 15. If the bulb lights, there is power in the circuit, so the problem is probably within the locomotive or accessory, requiring the services of a qualified repair person. But if the bulb does not light, the problem lies somewhere between the transformer and the track or accessory. Work your way back along the circuit, testing every point (terminal block, barrier strip, etc.) where wires are connected until you find a spot where the bulb lights. Then look for a loose connection, or possibly a broken wire, in that area. As a last resort, replace all of the wire in the circuit.

Wiring diagrams

Figure 16 is a schematic diagram of the track layout built from our Atlas starter set, showing power and ground wires from the transformer connected to the terminal track section. In addition, we have added an on/off toggle switch in the power circuit. In a simple layout such as this, the toggle switch isn't really needed, but since we will shortly be adding more track to expand operating possibilities, let's include the switch now, so it is there when we need it. (Instructions for installing circuits with toggle switches and other electrical connections are found in Chapter 6.)

The layout shown in the diagram represents Atlas track, with 12 sections of curved track (6 on each side) and 6 sections of straight track, 3 at the top and 3 at the bottom. A circle made up of 12 sections of Atlas track is approximately 36 inches in diameter, measured

between the middle rails. Lionel and MTH make similar track components. While they differ somewhat in construction, appearance, and the way the sections fit together, the same principles apply to all three systems with respect to wiring.

MTH RealTrax

The MTH RealTrax system consists of solid T-shaped rails (Atlas rails are hollow) that are mounted on black plastic ties surrounded by grey simulated ballast, 17. Eight curved sections make a full circle approximately 31" in diameter. Whereas all three rails in the Atlas system are shiny, the RealTrax middle rail is black. The plastic base is relatively heavy, and electrical connections between the sections are achieved by means of curved spring-loaded metal fingers.

Wires from the transformer connect to the track through a plug-in device, **18**. This connector is also referred to by the manufacturer as a lockon. A four-sided lantern on top has green lenses on all sides that light up when the current is turned on. Two plastic extensions on the box are fitted with thin metal plates, one of which makes the ground connection to an outside rail. The other extension joins to the middle rail for the power (throttle) connection. To attach the lockon to the track, you must first snap out a prescored rectangular slot in the side of the roadbed with a pair of pliers.

Photo **19** shows the underside of the track with the lockon inserted in the slot. The long extension passes beneath a thin metal plate connected to the middle rail, and the short extension slips under a plate connected to one outside rail. There are two ways to connect wires from the transformer, **20**. MTH provides a pair of cables fitted with right-angled plugs on one end, which may be inserted into the wire caps, on the sides of the lockon. Alternatively, if you partially unscrew the cap, it exposes a small round hole in the shaft. You can strip the insulation off the end of a wire and insert it into the hole and then screw the cap down tight for a secure connection.

Lionel FasTrack

The hollow U-shaped rails on Lionel's FasTrack sections, all of which are shiny, are fastened to the roadbed with metal tabs that pass through slots in the plastic base. The tabs are bent over on the underside to hold the rails in place, **21**. One end of each outer rail is fitted with a heavy metal pin that slides into the open end of the rail on an adjoining section. The middle rail is fitted with a shorter pin, which is only half as thick as the longer pins. When two sections are joined together, the short pins from both middle rails slide in next to each other for a secure electrical connection. Eight sections of curved track make up a full circle approximately 36" in diameter, measured over the outermost rails.

FasTrack sections do not use a lockon for wire connections from the

Wiring diagrams

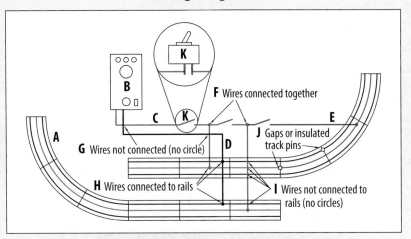

Certain conventions have been adopted for the schematic diagrams, such as figure 16, that appear throughout this book.

A. Track sections are shown with black ground rails and colored power (middle) rails. The colors of the middle rails match the wires attached to them. The roadbed (when present) is outlined thinly in black.

B. Transformer.

C. Track power wires are shown in color, according to the side of the circuit that they represent. The main power circuit is usually red, except when more than one throttle is employed.

D. All ground wires are black, even when two or more throttles are used.

E. Power wires in secondary circuits are shown in colors other than red, except in the case of accessories where the manufacturer has supplied a red wire.

F. Solid circles indicate that wires are connected together.

G. Wires that pass over each other without circles in the diagrams are not connected.

H. Solid circles indicate wires that are connected to rails.

I. No circles appear where wires pass under the rails without a connection.

J. Squares indicate gaps in the rails between sections of track or insulated track pins.

K. An on/off toggle switch (inset) is symbolized by an interrupted wire, as shown in the small circle to the right of the transformer, and at two subsequent points in that wire.

transformer. Instead, two wires are fitted with miniature slide-on connectors called *female quick-disconnect lugs* that slide onto narrow metal plates on the underside of the track, **22**. There is a small slot in the side of the roadbed that allows the wires to pass through to the transformer. On a permanent layout, you can thread the wires through a hole in the table instead, hiding them from sight.

Expanding a set

Straight out of the box, a toy train set is limited as to what you can do

with it. The locomotive can stop and start and run in a circle (both forward and backward). It smokes. The whistle blows, and the bell rings. But once the novelty wears off, there isn't much happening to maintain interest. That's when it's time to expand the basic set into a miniature railroad. The first addition most people consider is the purchase of more track to increase the distance traveled by the train and the number of routes it can take. We'll explore expanding a set into a layout in Chapter 3.

CHAPTER THREE

1

From train set to layout

Adding extra track sections, turnouts, crossings, and uncouplers (often sold in expansion packs) helps transform a train set into a layout.

The major manufacturers of O gauge trains offer various products for expanding a basic starter set into a miniature railroad, **1**. For example, Atlas sells three different expansion packs for its Industrial Rail sets, **2**. It contains a 90-degree crossing, six extra curved tracks, and four short straight sections to make a figure eight. Other sets provide sidings and alternate routes for a train to travel on. Lionel and MTH also sell a wide variety of extra track components for expanding a layout. The most common additions are turnouts, crossings, and operating track sections, or uncouplers.

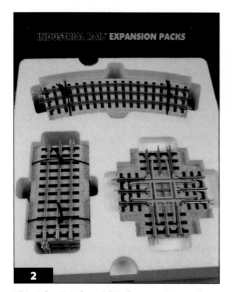

2

This Atlas O Industrial Rail expansion pack contains enough track to create a figure-eight design when added to a basic starter set.

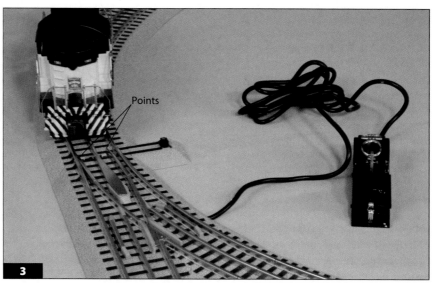

Points

3

Lionel's FasTrack turnouts are offered in manual and remote control versions. The latter are completely prewired at the factory. In this photo, the points of the turnout are turned to direct this foreshortened GP-7 diesel made by Ready Made Toys toward the curved rail side.

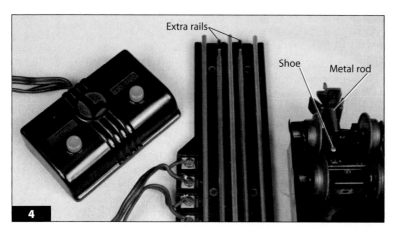

Extra rails

Shoe   Metal rod

4

The first Lionel remote control operating cars were introduced shortly before World War II, along with an operating track section that provided hands-free uncoupling.

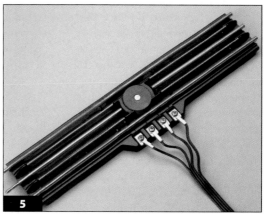

5

Postwar versions of Lionel's operating track section contain a central magnet for uncoupling.

Turnouts

A *turnout* is a track section that diverges into two routes by means of moveable rails called *points*, **3**. A manual turnout has a lever mounted on the base that can be thrown by hand to move the points. A remote control turnout, like the Lionel FasTrack model in the photo, is activated by a solenoid or miniature motor and has a control box attached to it by a cable. It derives its power from the track and requires no special wiring. Moving the lever on the control box shifts the points and directs the trains down the selected path.

Operating track sections

Lionel introduced the first remote control uncoupling system in 1938,

a major step forward in providing greater fun and operating possibilities, **4**. In its original form, the system was based on what Lionel called a Remote Control Track Set, more commonly referred to today as an *operating track section*. This device contains two extra rails located between the middle and outside rails. Between the wheels at each end of the car is a small plastic rectangle called a *shoe*, fitted with a metal stud in the center. This shoe rides along one of the extra rails as the car passes over the section. The control box features an uncouple button and an unload button. When you press the uncouple button, it connects the extra rails to the power side of the circuit. The electric current passes

from a rail to the shoe and then to an electromagnetic solenoid that moves a metal rod and causes the coupler to open. The solenoid is grounded through the wheels of the car.

Lionel introduced its first piece of remote control animated rolling stock in 1938, a coal dump car. There are two shoes underneath the car, staggered so that one rides on each of the extra rails. When you push the unload button, one shoe receives power and the other one is grounded. The current activates a solenoid in the car that tilts the bin and causes it to dump its load of coal. More than 70 years after this invention was introduced, some of Lionel's operating cars—log and coal dump cars, milk delivery cars, and a

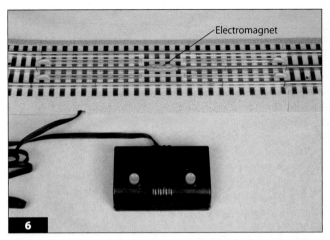

Electromagnet

This Lionel FasTrack operating section differs from vintage models in appearance, although the control box looks virtually identical. In fact, the mechanical components inside the box are also exactly the same as the original design (see photo 4).

Push the right-hand unload button, and the logs tumble into the waiting bin.

number of others—still operate the same way.

In 1948, Lionel introduced a simplified and less expensive uncoupling mechanism, in which an electromagnet is mounted in the middle of the operating track section, **5**. When the uncouple button is pushed, the magnet is energized and attracts a metal plate or disk on the underside of the car, pulling it down to open the coupler. This system evolved into the familiar *thumbtack coupler* (named after the appearance of the disk) that is used by most manufacturers today. This track section still contained the extra rails, as Lionel continued to install solenoid-operated couplers on some equipment, and they were also needed to operate dump cars and other pieces of animated rolling stock.

Lionel's recent FasTrack system features a five-rail operating track that functions similar to the 1948 design, with an unobtrusive narrow electromagnet mounted in the center, **6**. The log dump car in photo **7** is a recent product, based on a Lionel design that is more than half a century old. Parked over a modern FasTrack operating section, it would work just as well on an original 1938 or 1948 operating track or on an MTH or Atlas operating track.

Putting the components to use

By adding a turnout and some extra curved and straight track, including an operating track section for uncoupling, **8**, you can increase the operational potential of a basic loop of track to make running your trains more interesting. Figure **9** shows a layout built with Lionel's FasTrack components that adds a siding where a train can back up, uncouple from its cars, and return to the main line. This same layout can also be constructed with Atlas or MTH track, and it would be wired the same way.

Note that the wiring scheme has not changed from the simple loop of track in figure 2-16, except that we have replaced the Atlas terminal track with a Lionel section having the wires connected underneath the roadbed. This is indicated by the circles on the ends of the wires where they meet the rails. Just two wires, power and ground, are sufficient to power the entire layout. Because all of the rails are connected together by track pins, electricity is carried everywhere.

The layout now has increased operating possibilities. You can locate an industry (a building or an accessory) next to the siding to simulate the delivery of freight. The locomotive can leave its cars on the siding and return to the main line for a run, while workmen unload the cargo. The locomotive can then return to pick up the empty cars. To complete this expanded layout, let's add a bumper to keep cars from running off the end of the siding. Lionel's FasTrack system includes a molded plastic bumper unit that snaps onto any section of track. Also, to fit any avail-

able space, you can add extra straight sections to create longer runs.

Creating an insulated block

As shown in photo **10**, it is also possible to accommodate two trains on this layout, one sitting on the siding while the other circles the main line. However, the way the layout is wired creates a problem. Every time you advance the throttle to make the Atlas passenger train circle the layout, the diminutive Lionel diesel switcher on the siding also moves. The two engines cannot operate independently.

A wiring solution to this problem is isolating the middle rail of the siding electrically from the rest of the layout by leaving a gap in the middle rail between two sections of track, **11**. This can be accomplished in different ways depending upon which track products you use. You will need a new power wire from the transformer to the middle rail of the siding (shown in blue in the diagram) with an on/off toggle switch included in the circuit. If you turn on the main line (the red toggle switch) and turn off the siding (the blue toggle), you can run the passenger train while the freight train remains motionless on the siding. Turn both toggles the other way, and the passenger train stops while you run the diesel back and forth along the siding.

The siding is now referred to as a *block*, an area of track that is isolated from the rest of the layout electrically,

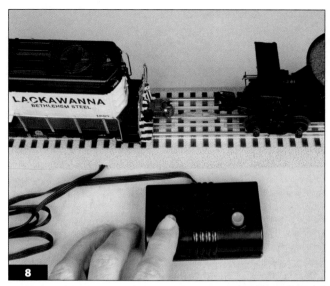

8

The uncouple button separates this Ready Made Toys Beep locomotive from its cars on a siding, which adds interest to running trains.

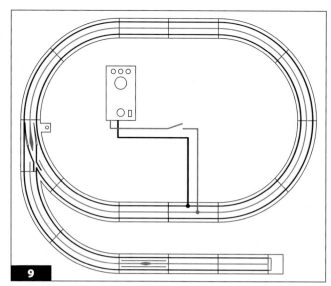

9

Adding a siding to a basic loop of track provides additional operating opportunities. A bumper rests at the end of the siding.

10

Two trains may operate independently on the same layout when the track is wired in blocks.

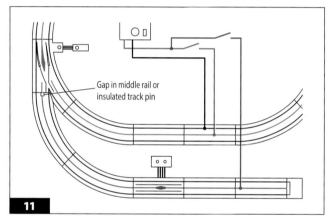

11

Gap in middle rail or insulated track pin

Isolating the middle rail of the siding creates a block.

and it is controlled by a toggle switch or other device. You can connect such a block to a separate throttle, or even to a second transformer, as described in Chapter 5.

Lionel traditional track. With traditional toy train track, you can prevent current from affecting the siding block by removing the round pin from the middle rail with a pair of pliers, **12**. When you connect the sections of track, don't push them together completely—make sure that a very small gap remains between the middle rails, so they don't touch each other. For a more dependable installation, insert a plastic insulating pin in the middle rail. Available from hobby stores or online, these pins have a raised collar that prevents the middle rails of the two sections of track from touching.

Atlas O. As of this writing, Atlas O does not make insulated track pins to fit the small rail openings of its Industrial Rail track system. However, suitable pins are available from GarGraves Trackage (www.gargraves.com) and from toy-train parts suppliers, **13**. These pins also fit Ross and GarGraves track, as well as Lionel Super O track from the 1950s.

Remove the small flat metal pin from the middle rail with pliers and replace it with an insulating pin. Insert the pin long end first. There is a small raised shoulder on the pin that keeps the end of the rail from touching the rail on an adjoining section of track.

If you decide not to purchase insulating pins, it is possible to leave the metal pin out of the middle rail, but because Atlas track snaps together

quite tightly, it is possible that even without the pin, the middle rails will touch each other and conduct electricity. To prevent this, place a small strip of black electrical tape over the end of one rail before assembling the track, **14**.

MTH RealTrax and Lionel FasTrack. If you are using MTH RealTrax or Lionel FasTrack, you can purchase track sections that allow you to interrupt the current flowing through the rails. MTH RealTrax sections are half the length of an ordinary section and have narrow breaks in all three rails, **15**. On the underside of the track, three jumper wires carry the current from one side to the other. To create an insulated track block, simply remove the jumper wire for the third rail.

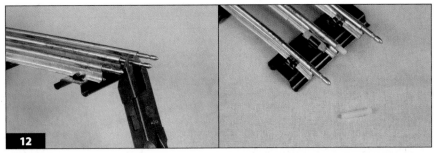

12

Plastic track pins replace the metal variety in the middle rail to create an insulated block.

13

GarGraves plastic track pins work well with Atlas Industrial Rail track to create an insulated block.

14

If you don't use an insulated plastic track pin, place a small strip of black electrical tape over the rail end.

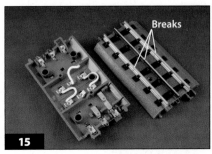

15

Breaks

The rails in this MTH insulated track section are interrupted in the middle. Underneath, the middle rail jumper wire has been partially disconnected to interrupt the current flow from one side of the rail to the other.

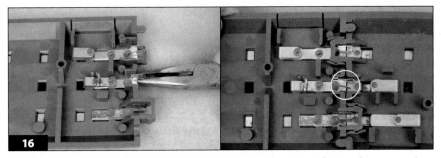

16

By pinching one middle rail connector, you can interrupt the current flow to the next section.

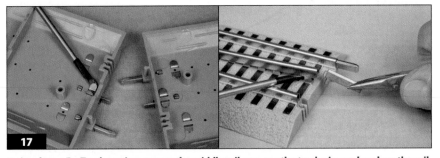

17

To insulate a FasTrack section, pry up the middle rail, remove the track pin, and replace the rail.

finger together with a pair of pliers and connect the section to another piece of track, **16**. Make sure they do not touch each other when the sections are connected. The middle rails themselves will probably not touch each other, but if they do, separate them with a small strip of electrical tape, as in photo **14**.

Insulating a Lionel FasTrack section requires a bit more work, and is probably not worth the effort unless you have a great number of blocks. You will have to remove the track pins from the middle rails of both sections where they meet. On the underside of the roadbed, pry up the two metal tabs that hold the middle rail in place with a thin-bladed screwdriver, **17**.

Turn the track over. Insert the screwdriver under one side of the rail and pry it up just enough to allow you to remove the metal pin. Then fit the rail back into the slots in the roadbed and bend the metal tabs back in place. Do the same thing to the adjoining track section so that there are no pins in either middle rail. Because FasTrack sections fit together tightly, you should place a small strip of electrical tape between the rails, similar to the procedure used when modifying Atlas and MTH track sections.

We now have the beginning of a true model railroad, with a main line and a storage siding properly wired so that two trains may operate independently. However, there is still one limitation to our enjoyment of the layout. There is no easy way for the train on the main line and the train on the siding to change places. We will address this issue in Chapter 4.

The MTH RealTrax Insulated Straight Track Section Set (40-1029) includes two 5" sections. The Lionel FasTrack product is the Block Section (6-12060). With both of these products it is possible to insulate the outer rails as well as the middle one. Insulated outside rails can be used to operate trackside accessories, as explained in Chapter 8.

If you have many track blocks on your layout, you may wish to save some money by modifying the ends of two track sections where they meet, instead of buying these special track sections. This is relatively easy to accomplish with MTH RealTrax. At the middle rail location on one track section, squeeze the springy metal

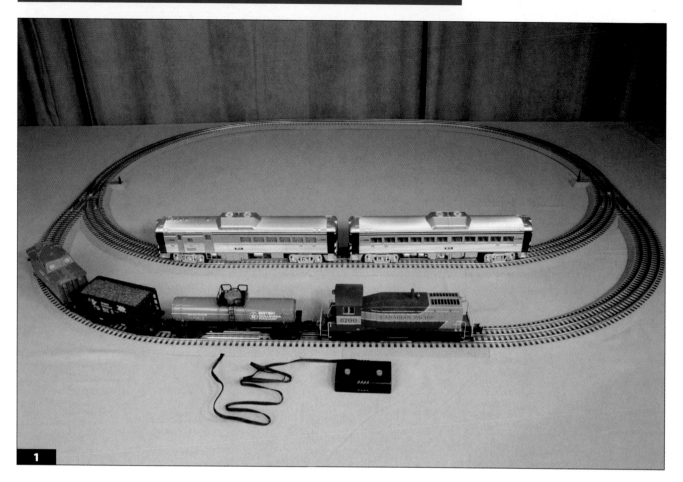

CHAPTER FOUR

1

Expanding a layout

No single track component is more important than the turnout for creating an interesting layout, and we'll explore its versatility as we expand our basic loop-and-siding railroad into a miniature empire. Using one turnout, we added a stub siding to the layout in the previous chapter. (A stub siding has only one point of entry and stops in a dead end.) In this chapter, we'll continue to expand the layout by adding another turnout to create a passing siding, so called because it allows two trains to pass each other, **1**.

A simple loop of track can become an elaborate layout with the addition of turnouts and other track components. Here, a passing siding makes two-train operation possible.

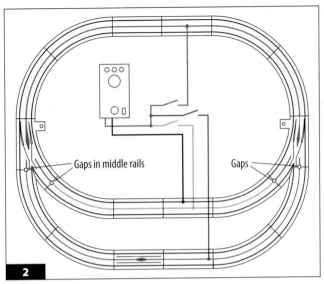

2

This layout has four locations where there are gaps in the middle rail or insulated track pins installed.

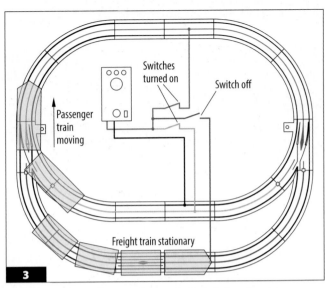

3

With the passing siding switch turned off, and the other two switches on, only the passing siding has no power.

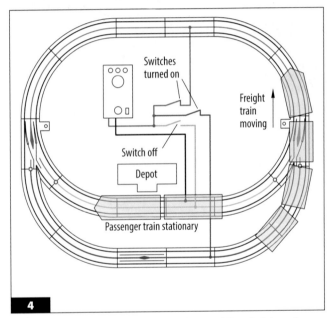

4

You can stop a passenger train at the depot, while a freight train runs on the outer loop.

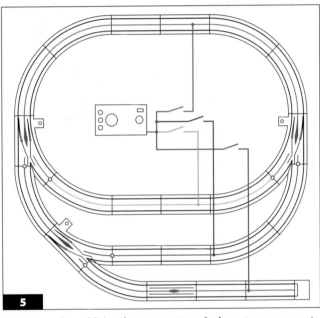

5

By adding a few additional components to the layout, you can create a stub siding for storing your rolling stock.

Passing sidings

Turnouts are labeled according to the direction taken by the curved portion. A left-hand turnout, like the one first installed in Chapter 3, causes a locomotive to turn to the left. To make a passing siding, we'll add a right-hand turnout at the opposite side of the layout. (For purposes of illustration, the layouts shown in this chapter are relatively compact, with just two sections of straight track on the long sides of the loop and the passing siding. The layout may be extended in any direction by adding extra straight track.)

The wiring for a layout with a passing siding is a bit more complicated than for a stub siding, but the extra effort pays big dividends in terms of operation, **2**. The mainline power wire is shown in red on the diagram, with the attachment point relocated to the top of the layout. A second wire, the orange one, powers the inside part of the loop, and a blue wire is connected to the middle rail of the passing siding. There are now three blocks of track, each with a separate toggle switch to turn them on or off. Take special note of the four locations where

there are gaps in the middle rail, or insulated track pins are installed.

Photo **1** shows the layout with two trains running on it. The passenger train on the inside track is a set of MTH rail diesel cars in British Columbia Railroad livery. An Atlas Canadian Pacific switcher pulling three Lionel freight cars with Canadian road names sits on the passing siding.

The wiring arrangement in figure **3** shows the passing siding toggle switch turned off and the other two switches turned on so that power reaches all

6

O gauge trains from different manufacturers are basically compatible and can be used together on the same layout no matter what brand of track you have. Coupler height and size, the amount of voltage needed to operate the motors, similar smoke units, compatible whistle and bell circuits, and identical wheel gauge are just some of the features that allow you to mix and match equipment.

the track except for the passing siding. This allows the passenger train to circle the mainline loop via the inner track when the turnouts are set to the curved position, while the freight train stands still.

In figure **4**, we have placed a passenger depot beside the inner part of the main line to give the rail diesel cars a destination. Bring the passenger train to a halt in front of the depot and turn off the toggle switch for the inner part of the loop (the orange wire). Turn on the passing siding switch (blue) and also throw both of the turnouts to the straight position. With power going to the outer half of the main line and the passing siding, the freight train can now circle the perimeter of the layout.

The next step in our expansion project is to add several more track components to make a stub siding for storage: one more turnout, some additional straight track, and a bumper, **5**. We will also relocate the operating track section from the passing siding to the stub siding so that cars may be uncoupled and left there. (Of course, you can also leave the operating track in the passing siding and purchase another one for the stub siding.)

Wiring for the stub siding is shown in green. Note the location of the gap or insulated pin between the turnout

and the siding. Remember that when wires are shown crossing each other in these diagrams, there is no connection between them unless there is a circle at the junction. There are now four toggle switches to control the layout, two for the main line (red and orange), one for the passing siding (blue), and one for the stub siding (green). Any or all of them may be turned on or off at any time to facilitate train movements.

It is possible to place three locomotives on the layout, although they will appear to be very crowded. In that case, you can make the layout bigger and more realistic by adding additional straight track for longer runs. We equipped this layout for the Pennsylvania Railroad, with a late 19th century Consolidation locomotive and a vintage coach on the main line (probably a railfan trip), **6**.

The freight train on the passing siding is headed by two Pennsylvania boxcab electric engines that are pulling three freight cars from the neighboring Lancaster and Chester Railroad. The steamer and coach are MTH products, and the remaining pieces are Lionel products from different eras. The GG-1 locomotive on the stub siding is a recent Lionel reissue of its original 2332 that was introduced in 1948.

Organizing the wiring

As a layout grows in size and complexity, it becomes important to gain control of the wiring and assemble it in an economical fashion. The two basic principles are (1) use the minimum amount of wire to achieve the necessary connections, and (2) plan ahead to make access for repairs and upgrades as easy as possible.

The first step is to provide for more track connections. While you can continue to use terminal track sections or lockons wherever required, it isn't really necessary to go to the extra expense. Also, terminal sections and lockons are not realistic, and hidden wiring greatly improves the appearance of a layout.

It is not difficult or expensive to connect wires directly to the underside of the track. To start, cut two 6" wires, one red for power and one black for ground, and strip a ¼" of insulation from both ends. Crimp a miniature U-shaped lug on one end of each wire, using the jaws of a handheld wire stripper, **7**. These lugs are available from any electronics supply store.

To connect these wires to a piece of traditional toy train track, insert a medium-sized screwdriver blade into the slot in the bottom of the rail and apply a bit of pressure to widen the gap slightly, **8**. Force the lug into the gap. Don't open the slot too much, as you want the rail to hold the lug tightly. This method also works with GarGraves and Ross track (see Chapter 10). Put the red wire in the middle rail and the black wire in one of the outside rails to help you identify the power and ground wires later when working underneath the layout table.

These U-shaped lugs can also be used to connect wires to MTH RealTrax, **9**. The metal plates at the end of a section are held in place by plastic rods that project outward from the roadbed. Slip the lugs under the top part of the plate and around the rod. You will have to bend the lugs somewhat to make them fit. Position them in such a way that they are held firmly in place between the plates and the plastic supports under the roadbed. You may have to experiment

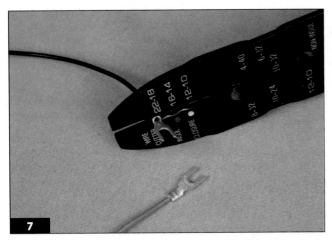

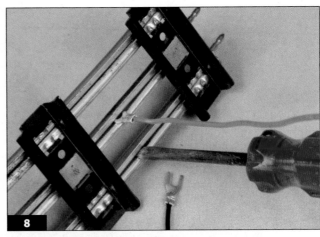

7 Use a handheld wire stripper to clamp a spade lug onto the end of a wire.

8 Instead of using a lockon, you can conceal wires by placing an electrical lug into the slot on the bottom of a section of track.

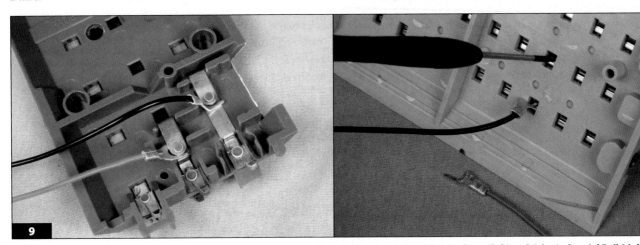

9 Using these simple lugs, it is possible to hide the wiring under every brand of track, such as MTH RealTrax (left) and Atlas Industrial Rail (right).

a bit to determine how much to bend the lugs to achieve a tight fit.

To connect wires underneath a piece of Atlas Industrial Rail track, cut off one side of each lug, **9**. Open up the slot on the underside of the rail very slightly with a narrow-bladed screwdriver, and force the remaining half of the lug into the slot. As with traditional track, don't open up the rail any more than is necessary to insert the lug in order to maintain a tight connection.

For Lionel FasTrack, you can make your own wire connections exactly like those sold by the company but at much less cost. Purchase a package of small female quick-disconnect lugs from an electronics supply store. Crimp one to a wire and slide it onto the metal plate for the center rail on the underside of the track, **10**. You can use another quick-disconnect lug to attach a ground wire to the outside rail plate.

To install the wires on the layout, drill holes in the table for them to pass through. Strip about a ¼" of insulation from the end of each wire. Insert them into a two-position terminal block, **11**. Secure the wires in the terminal block by tightening the small screws in the round openings in the top of the block with a miniature screwdriver. Although this photo does not show it, remember that the table is between the track and the terminal blocks, which are located under the layout.

Terminal blocks come in a variety of sizes from electronics supply stores in strips of 8 or 12 positions. You can cut off as many as you need with a small saw—a hobby razor saw works best.

Mount the terminal block on the underside of the layout table with a screw through the hole between the two positions. Then connect the ground and power wires from the transformer to the opposite side of the

terminal as shown. Note that on the side of the terminal block where the ground wire from the track is connected, another ground wire emerges. This is called a *bus wire*, as explained in the following paragraphs. The openings in these terminal blocks are large enough to accept two, three, or even more wires, as you will see in later chapters.

Bus wire ground circuit

Both wire and track rails exhibit a certain amount of resistance to the passage of electricity, which can cause a locomotive to slow down when far away from the transformer. As the size of a layout increases, it is advisable to connect the ground wires to the track in two or more locations to avoid a voltage drop. There is also a certain amount of voltage drop caused by the mechanical connections between track sections (rail joiners or

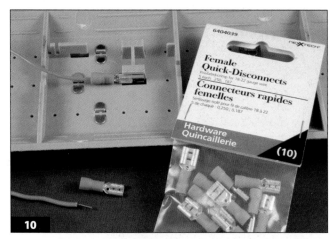

These packaged quick-disconnect female lugs are similar to the ones on a FasTrack system. Two size connectors are sometimes packaged together. The smaller size is the correct one to use with FasTrack.

Terminal blocks help keep your wiring neat and well organized, and they facilitate the removal of the wires whenever repairs or changes to the layout are made.

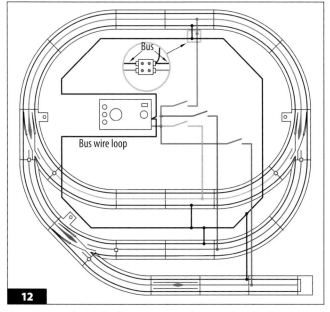

This diagram shows the bus wire ground connections for the inner loop, passing siding, and stub siding.

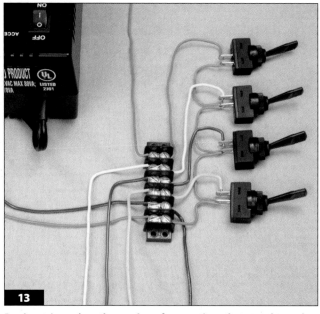

Barrier strips reduce the number of connections that must be made directly to the transformer.

track pins). By running extra wires to distant points, you can avoid this problem. (Another cause of voltage drop is inadequate wire size, which is discussed in Chapter 5.)

Begin by adding extra ground connections throughout the layout, one for each location where power wires are connected. To do this, install a continuous loop of ground wire all around the perimeter of the layout, **12**. This is commonly called a bus wire. The power and ground wires are connected to the rails at the top of the diagram. The ground wire from the rail is connected through a plastic terminal block to the bus wire, and the power wire is

connected to the transformer through the other side of the terminal block, as shown in the inset. The bus wire extends in both directions.

The connections for the inner loop, passing siding, and stub siding are constructed in the same manner. The diagram shows all of the bus wire ground connections. The power connections are shown attached directly to the transformer for simplicity, but all of these connections should be routed through terminal blocks.

Larger layouts with many blocks need careful organization where wires emerge from the transformer. The best device for this job is a barrier

strip, **13**. A barrier strip is a plastic terminal device fitted with pairs of screws on the surface that are connected together electrically. There are small raised plastic fences (barriers) between the pairs to prevent adjacent wires from touching each other.

It is much easier to connect multiple wires to a barrier strip than to the posts of a transformer. Connect just one wire from each transformer post to a screw on one side of the barrier strip. Connect all of the layout wires to the opposite side of the strip. Using barrier strips ensures that future maintenance or layout changes will be simplified. For example, suppose you want to

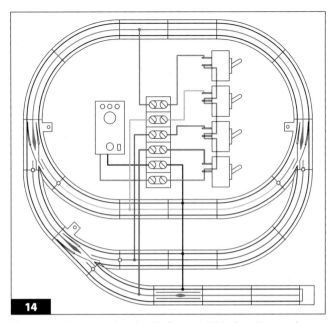

14

You can make connections for the four track blocks using toggle switches and a six-position barrier strip.

15

Accessories such as this MTH transfer dock bring action and visual appeal to even the simplest of layouts.

16

On the transfer dock, clips A and B are the power and ground connections for the conveyor motor, and clips C and D are power and ground for the lights. The track power and accessory power connections to an Atlas transformer are shown at right. Speaker wire, the type made for connecting audio components, works well on a model railroad.

exchange your starter-set transformer for a larger, more powerful model. If all of your wiring—every track block, every accessory, every signal—is attached directly to the transformer, you will have a huge number of wires to sort out. If, however, there are only three wires (track power, accessory power, and ground) leading from the transformer to a barrier strip, you will only have to disconnect three wires and reconnect them to the new transformer. None of the track and accessory wires will be disturbed.

Also, if wires must be soldered to the toggle switches, it will be easier to replace a switch or make other

changes if those wires are screwed to a barrier strip, rather than extended all the way to a track connection at some distant point.

Figure **14** illustrates the connections for the four track blocks in our expanded layout using toggle switches and a six-position barrier strip. The same arrangement appears in photo **13**, ready to be installed on a control panel, as described in Chapter 6. The wires are color-coded for identification of circuits. (While some of the colors in the photo differ from those in the diagram, they are consistent from side to side of the barrier strip.)

Adding an accessory

Before expanding the layout further, let's add an action accessory, such as the MTH transfer dock, **15**, which makes use of the accessory circuit or circuits found on most transformers. This large building contains two motorized conveyor belts that move from side to side. Miniature figures attached to the belts travel back and forth carrying products and pushing handcarts. The building is also lighted. The loading ramp is at the proper height for use with MTH operating box and refrigerator cars.

There are four Fahnestock clips on the underside where wires are to be

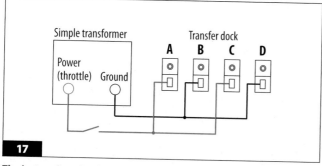

17

The instructions for the accessory dock provide this method for wiring the dock to the transformer.

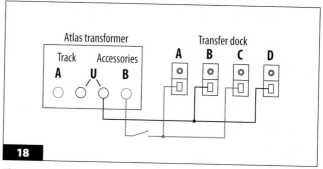

18

This Atlas transformer has a separate accessory circuit, which provides more consistent operation.

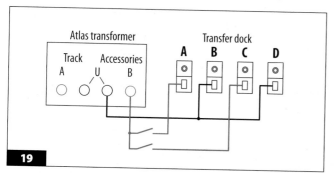

19

To keep the light on when the belts are off, add a second switch and a separate wire from C on the dock to accessory power post B.

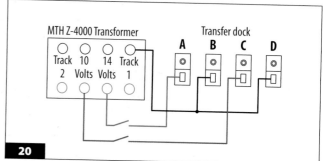

20

A pair of toggle switches will turn both circuits on and off.

connected, **16**. These are labeled A, B, C, and D from left to right. Clips A and B are the power and ground connections for the conveyor motor. Clips C and D are power and ground for the lights.

The transfer dock operates well with any transformer. The instruction booklet that comes with this accessory gives one very simple method for installing the wiring, but in fact, there are several options available, depending upon how you want the dock to operate. Figure **17** shows the method described in the instructions, which is suitable for any transformer, even the simplest ones that have no separate accessory circuit. I have added a toggle switch in the power line so that the dock may be turned off while the train is running. Without the switch, the dock will always be working whenever there is power in the track.

If the dock is located some distance from the transformer, you can connect it directly to the track instead. Attach the power wires (clips A and C) to the middle rail and the ground wires (B and D) to one of the outside rails.

There are a few disadvantages to this wiring arrangement. If the train is

stopped with the power off, the dock will not operate, so you must leave a stationary locomotive in neutral with the throttle advanced for the action to continue. And because the voltage in the track goes up and down as the throttle is used to change the speed of the train, the light inside the building will brighten and dim correspondingly. The motor will also run faster and slower as the train speeds up and slows down. A transformer with a separate accessory circuit, such as the Atlas model diagrammed in figure **18**, provides more consistent operation.

The accessory circuit of the Atlas transformer may be set to any voltage between 6 and 16. The transfer dock operates well at about 14 volts, but other settings may be chosen to make the figures move faster or slower. Whenever the toggle switch is on, the light will also be on and the figures will travel back and forth, but it is also possible to have the light on when the conveyor belts are not operating. Just add a second toggle switch and a separate wire from the light connection (C on the dock) to the accessory power post B on the transformer, **19**.

The MTH Z-4000 Transformer does not have a variable voltage circuit for accessories. Instead, there are two fixed voltage posts, one providing 10 volts and the other 14 volts. These two ranges are ideal for accessories such as the transfer dock. The 14-volt circuit runs the motor at a moderate speed, and the 10-volt circuit provides a realistic level of lighting for this type of industrial building. Connect the wires as shown in figure **20**, including a pair of toggle switches to turn both circuits on and off.

Lionel's ZW Transformer has two variable voltage posts. You can connect the motor of the transfer dock to one post and the lights to the other post and adjust them to provide whatever level of conveyor belt speed and amount of light you want.

One train running on a layout can be fun, but operating two or more trains simultaneously can make the difference between simply owning a train set and commanding a model railroad empire. To achieve multi-train operation, we need to have independent control of the trains with separate throttles, as addressed in Chapter 5.

CHAPTER FIVE

1

Operating with multiple throttles

Two trains thundering past each other, each controlled by its own independent throttle, will more than double the fun of operating a layout.

Although the layout we have built so far can accommodate two trains, we cannot operate them both at the same time at different speeds. To overcome this limitation, let's redesign the layout to include two full loops of track and also add a second transformer, **1**. The revised layout is divided into two blocks, one for each loop, **2**. Power is provided by two Atlas transformers. One is connected to the outer loop (blue) and the other to the inner loop (red). The transformer for the blue line affects only the train running on that loop of track. The other transformer operates only the red line train.

Common ground

Examine the ground wire (black). There is only one ground circuit for the entire layout, arranged as a bus wire connected to both transformers and to all of the outside rails in both loops at four locations. This is called a *common ground*, which is the most efficient and economical method of wiring a layout. The ground and power wire connections to the track are adjacent to each other, routed through terminal blocks as explained in Chapter 4.

Since there are only two separate blocks, just two toggle switches are required for this layout design. But in order to prevent voltage drop, we have connected the power wires from each transformer to its loop of track at two widely separated locations. This ensures that each train will maintain a constant speed everywhere on its loop. The wires will be routed from a barrier strip instead of from the toggles, **3**.

Note that the toggle switches have just two wires soldered to them. But if we did not use a barrier strip, we would have to solder one more wire to each one in order to install two wire connections to the opposite sides of both loops. And if the layout were quite large, requiring four connections to the middle rail of each loop to prevent voltage drop, the number of wires soldered to each switch would become unwieldy. By using a barrier strip, these connections are all made easily with a screwdriver, and are just as easily disconnected if it should become necessary for maintenance or repair.

In two places, the wires going to the track are attached to the same side of the barrier strip as the wires from the toggles (the blue wires at the top of the strip and the red wires at the bottom position). It doesn't matter which side you use—choose the one that is closest to where you want the wire to go.

About wire size

An important consideration when building a large layout is the size of the wire used to power the track, **4**. The thickness of a wire is expressed as its gauge, a numerical figure in which

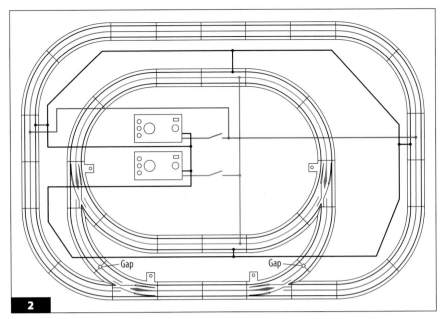

2

The gaps in the middle rails are located in the connector tracks between the pairs of turnouts.

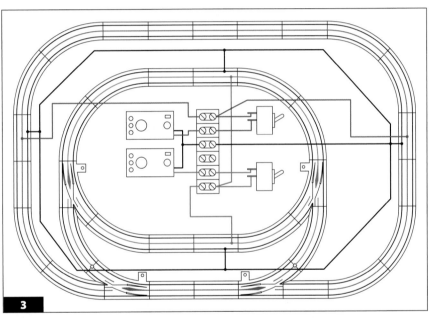

3

The wiring may look complicated, but this is actually the most efficient way of organizing it.

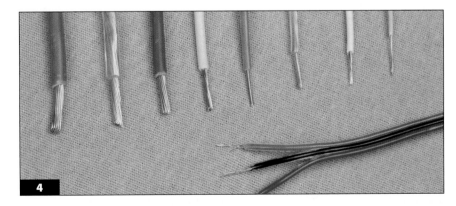

4

Common wires range from 10 gauge (left) to 24 gauge (right). The red wire in the center has a solid core, the others are stranded. The 24 gauge, three-wire cable is the type supplied with turnouts and signals, where the low level of current precludes a voltage-drop problem.

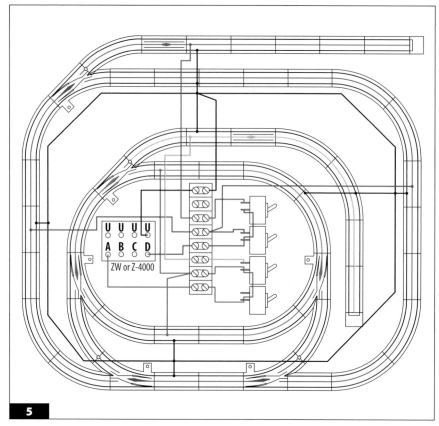

5

The expanded layout includes one storage siding for each loop. The sidings feature bumpers at the ends and operating track sections.

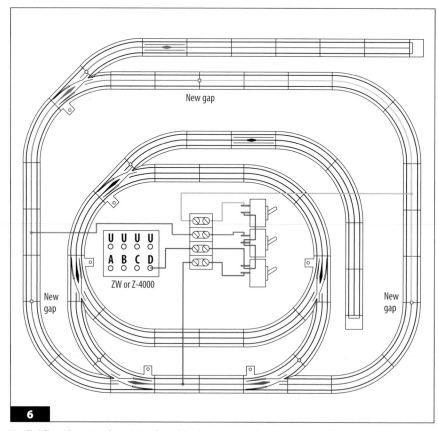

6

By dividing the outer loop into three blocks, you can shut down part of the line while using an accessory or moving a train onto a siding.

lower numbers denote thicker wires and higher numbers indicate thinner ones. A typical starter train set comes with relatively short lengths of 18 gauge wire for use between the transformer and the track. This is perfectly adequate for a small layout.

As more track is added, however, and especially when long pieces of wire must be used to connect to distant points on a layout, heavier wire is needed—16 gauge for medium-size layouts and 14 gauge for room-sized pikes. Huge layouts may even use 12 gauge wire. Heavier wire has less resistance to the flow of electricity, thus reducing the possibility of voltage drop and preventing trains from slowing down when far away from the transformer.

Stranded wire is preferred over the solid core variety, as it is much more flexible and easier to work with. An auto supply outlet is a good source for reasonably inexpensive stranded wire in thicker sizes. For signals and accessories, however, and for turnouts and uncoupling ramps, lightweight wire (20, 22, or 24 gauge) is perfectly adequate. (Stereo speaker wire comes in these sizes from electronics supply stores.)

Two throttles, one transformer

Large layouts consume a lot of power. While having two separate transformers on a moderately sized layout works very well, there are several advantages to purchasing a single large transformer as a layout grows. The MTH Z-4000 and the Lionel ZW each contain two throttles in a single case plus two circuits for accessories. Output is very high, 400 watts for the Z-4000 and anywhere from 180 to 720 watts for the ZW, depending upon how many power supply modules you use. Either transformer can run multiple trains simultaneously along with a wide range of accessories and lights.

In addition to showing the installation of a large two-throttle transformer, figure **5** shows the layout expanded to include two storage sidings, one for each loop. Both sidings have bumpers at the ends and operating track sections for uncoupling and operating animated cars. The ground circuit is a simple bus wire, and there is a longer barrier strip to accommodate the extra wiring.

Extra track blocks

The layout shown so far in this chapter has just four track blocks, one for each loop and one for each siding. However, it is often advantageous to divide a large loop into two or more separate blocks, giving you the option to shut down part of the line while using an accessory or shunting a train onto a siding. Figure **6** shows the outer loop divided into three blocks (red, orange, and blue). Note the positions where gaps or insulated pins are located in the middle rail. (Wires to the inner loop and both sidings have been omitted from this diagram for clarity, as has the ground circuit bus wire.)

Command control

An MTH DCS command control system may be added to an existing layout at any time, without giving up the advantages of having the layout divided into blocks. Figure **7** shows how simple this installation can be when applied to our two-loop, two-siding layout. The left diagram shows the conventional wiring system from figure **5**. The right diagram shows the same system, but it is connected to just one throttle of the transformer through the MTH Track Interface Unit (TIU). For simplicity, the wires that lead to the track blocks are not shown in this view.

The new wiring is shown as thick dashed lines. Wires that have been eliminated are shown as thin dotted lines. It should now be apparent why the use of barrier strips is recommended to connect all of the wires on a layout. These few changes are easily made with a screwdriver, and there are no changes to be made to the wires soldered to the toggle switches or the wires that go to the various track blocks. The numbers in circles on the diagram refer to the following steps:

1. Remove the wires from transformer throttle posts A and D and ground post U (dotted lines) that go directly to the barrier strip.

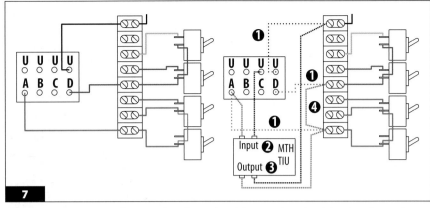

At left, the layout is wired conventionally, and at right, one throttle of the transformer is connected through the MTH Track Interface Unit.

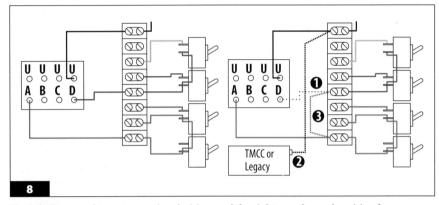

The left diagram shows conventional wiring, and the right one shows the wiring for command control.

2. Connect throttle post A and ground post U (dashed lines) to the TIU input terminals.
3. Connect the TIU output terminals to the power and ground positions on the barrier strip.
4. Connect the red power position on the barrier strip to the blue power position, which was formerly connected to the second throttle (transformer post D).

To operate with DCS command control, advance the throttle to approximately 18 volts and use the handheld controller. Power will now be routed to the entire layout from the transformer through the DCS module, but you still have the option of turning any of the track blocks on or off.

Lionel's TrainMaster command control or the new Legacy system may also be connected easily to the existing layout, **8**. The left diagram shows the original wiring, and the right one shows the command control wiring. As in the MTH example, new wires are shown dashed, while a dotted line represents the one wire that must be removed. The numbers in circles on the diagram refer to these steps:

1. Eliminate the wire from transformer throttle post D (dotted line) that goes directly to the barrier strip.
2. Connect a ground wire from the TMCC or Legacy unit to the ground position on the barrier strip.
3. Connect the red power position on the barrier strip to the blue power position, which was formerly connected to the second throttle (transformer post D).

To operate with TMCC or Legacy command control, advance the throttle to approximately 18 volts and use the handheld controller. Power will now be routed to the entire layout from one throttle of the transformer, but you still have the option of turning any of the track blocks on or off.

Both the MTH and Lionel command control systems come with comprehensive operating instructions,

Placing transformers in phase

North American households are provided with alternating current, in which the positive and negative poles alternate 60 times each second. In order to use two transformers together on one layout, the current reaching them both must alternate in unison, a condition called *being in phase*. If they are out of phase, it creates a perpetual overload.

Modern transformers have polarized wall plugs, in which one blade of the plug is wider than the other. They cannot be plugged into the wall socket incorrectly, and because the internal wiring of transformers is standardized across the industry, they will always be in phase with each other. However, if you use transformers that lack polarized plugs, such as those made by Lionel or American Flyer some decades ago, there's a 50–50 chance that they will be out of phase when plugged in.

To place two vintage transformers in phase, connect a wire from the ground post of one to the ground post of the other. (See chart on page 13 to identify ground posts.) Connect a wire to the throttle post of one of the transformers. Plug in the two transformers and advance the throttles of both of them to about the halfway point (12–14 volts). Briefly touch the free end of the power wire to the throttle post of the second transformer. If there is a strong spark, the transformers are out of phase. Unplug one of the transformers and rotate its wall plug 180 degrees before plugging it back in. Now repeat the process of touching the power wire to the throttle post. There should be no spark, which means the transformers are in phase. Both may now be wired to a common ground. When phasing a modern transformer and a vintage one, only the plug on the older model will be reversible.

Most older transformers do not have an on/off switch and must be unplugged when not in use. To avoid having to phase them every time you plug them back in, you can paint a small white dot next to the left blade of each plug to remind you which way to insert them into the wall socket. Or an even better way is to plug them both into a power strip with an on/off switch, so that they will never have to be unplugged.

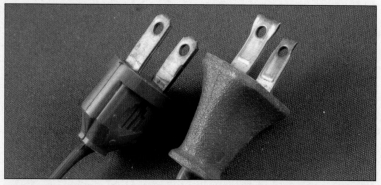

Modern transformers have polarized wall plugs (right) with one blade wider than the other. They can only be plugged into a wall socket one way. Vintage transformers do not have polarized plugs (left) and can be inserted into a wall socket with either blade in either slot.

To test if transformers are in phase, touch the free end of one transformer's power wire to the throttle post of the second transformer. If there is not a strong spark, the transformers are in phase.

By painting a small white dot next to the left blade of a plug, you'll know how to insert it correctly into the wall socket.

which are beyond the scope of this book. Command control systems are constructed from sophisticated solid-state electronics that may be easily damaged by overload conditions, including especially short circuits. It is essential that they be protected with fast-acting circuit breakers, such as those contained in modern transformers. If you are using an older model transformer, such as an original Lionel ZW or one of the other Lionel or American Flyer postwar units, install an external circuit breaker or a fast-blow fuse rated at 15 amps between the transformer and the DCS unit or between the transformer and the track when using TMCC or Legacy.

The next step in wiring a model railroad involves placing the toggle switches and other controls in a logical arrangement on a control panel, which is discussed in Chapter 6.

CHAPTER SIX

1

Organizing a control panel

The heart of a model railroad is its control center, the place where an operator can command the speed of the trains, choose the routes they will follow, and access features such as sound effects, uncoupling, and accessory activation, **1**.

There are various ways to construct a control panel. Whichever method you choose, it is important that the controls be organized in a logical pattern so that they can be identified quickly and easily. When two trains are approaching the same junction, you don't want to guess at which switch to throw in order to avoid a collision.

Easy-to-use controls make operating a layout more fun.

Dedicated switches such as these work well, but they take up a lot of space.

Clockwise from the bottom, commonly used on/off switches include a slide switch, a pair of miniature toggle switches, a pair of automotive toggle switches, and a pair of automotive rocker switches.

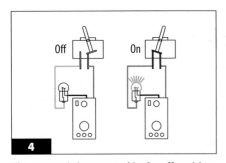

The current is interrupted in the off position (left) and passes through the switch in the on position (right) to light the bulb.

Four on/off rocker switches are labeled for the track blocks that they control. The one at left (the main line) is turned on. At right are controllers that came with Atlas turnouts.

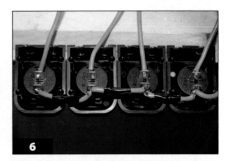

The blue wire is from the transformer's power post and is soldered to a connection point on each rocker switch through the red and black jumper wires. The red wires soldered to the other connection points lead to track blocks.

When constructing a control panel, you can group the controls according to function and add descriptive labels. Another way is to mount all the control switches on a graphic representation of the track plan. Or you may wish to decentralize the controls by locating accessory switches close to the devices they operate. This last method of organization is especially useful if you want visitors to the layout to operate the accessories themselves. There are advantages to each of these systems.

Also, you should consider whether to use the dedicated switches that come with track components and accessories, **2**. These devices work well and require a minimum of wiring, but they take up a lot of room on a control panel. Nevertheless, for a small layout, they are convenient and involve very little extra cost. In addition to the control switches pro-

vided by the manufacturer, you will need to buy a few on/off switches and associated hardware to control the various blocks of track.

Switches come in a variety of sizes and configurations, depending upon their intended uses. They may be purchased from many sources: most commonly, hardware, auto, and electronics supply stores; catalogs; and online sites. The most important consideration in choosing switches is their capacity. For connections to track, switches capable of handling 6–10 amps are a good choice. This power rating is well in excess of the current draw of even the largest locomotives. Switches rated at 2–5 amps are more than adequate for accessories and lights.

Basic on/off switches

A variety of simple on/off switches can be used on a toy train layout including automotive-type toggle

switches, automotive-type rocker switches, slide switches, and miniature toggle switches, **3**. Slide switches are often packaged with a toy train accessory, and miniature toggle switches are especially well suited for use on a graphic control panel, as explained on page 46.

Each of these switches has two connection points for wires. As an example, figure **4** shows how to connect a lightbulb to a transformer through an on/off toggle switch. The black wire is the ground connection, the red wire is the power connection, and the orange wire represents the power connection to the bulb before the toggle switch is turned on. Slide switches and rocker switches operate the same way, by moving an internal component to bridge the gap between the two electrical connection points. These types of switches are ideal for turning track blocks on and off.

The carousel and the park animations are connected to the accessory circuit of the transformer through on/off switches.

Simple control panel

A simple panel can control a small layout, for example, one having four track blocks, five turnouts, an uncoupler, and a few accessories. For this type of control panel, rocker switches are a compact solution to wiring track blocks, **5**. These automotive-type switches come with mounting brackets, so you can hang them under the edge of a layout. You can make identifying labels for the switches with a handheld electronic label maker from an office supply store, print the labels on a computer, or simply write them by hand.

Most toggle and rocker switches require soldered connections. To wire the rocker switches, solder the wire from the power post of the transformer to one connection point and connect it to each of the rocker switches through jumper wires, **6**. Then solder wires on the other connection points that lead to the track blocks. (See page 91 for effective soldering techniques.)

I mounted five compact, slide-switch controllers that came with Atlas turn-

outs next to the rocker switches by screwing them directly to the wooden molding that surrounds the layout. If you use Lionel or MTH turnouts, their controllers are larger and take up more room, but on a small layout like this, that is not a problem. (More information about Atlas and other turnout controllers appears in Chapter 10.)

A main feature of my layout is an amusement park that is operated by a few switches and two dedicated control boxes, **7**. Miniature toggle switches take up the least amount of room on a control panel. I used three miniature toggle switches and two push buttons, all of which fit into ¼" holes drilled into the molding around the layout. Two of the toggles operate the K-Line carousel and a variety of Lionel animated accessories such as miniature golf and playground swings. A third switch turns on the lights inside the buildings. The push buttons operate a water tower and the uncoupler track.

Next to these switches, I located the control box for an MTH operat-

ing passenger station, followed by the controller for a Lionel amusement park swing ride, **8**. On the other side of these controllers, I added another miniature toggle switch that turns an American Flyer log loader on and off. The easiest way to mount the control boxes on the side of a layout is with double-face tape. This specialized tape is sticky on both sides. Simply put a strip of tape on the back of the box and press it against the molding. Be sure to use removable tape, so you can peel it off cleanly if you decide to make changes later.

A few other accessories are scattered around this relatively small layout, and I chose to locate their controls close to them, rather than near the main control panel, **9**. This allows visitors (such as my grandchildren) to have a close-up view of the action while putting the accessories through their paces. However, on my other layout, I use a total of 42 switches to handle the large number of train and accessory operations. These switches are grouped together at a

Sometimes dedicated control boxes work best with complex accessories, such as the MTH animated station controller and the Lionel controller for the musical swing ride. At left, in ¼" holes, are three miniature toggle switches and two push buttons that control various components. At right is the on/off switch for an American Flyer log loader.

If you want your visitors to operate the accessories themselves, locate the control switches along the perimeter of the layout for easy access.

Grouping control switches in one area reduces the amount of wiring needed to connect them to the transformer.

centralized location with each switch labeled as to its function, **10**.

Common types of switches

The larger and more complex a layout becomes, the more you may wish to have a control panel that places the various switches within an illustration of the track plan. For an uncluttered and professional-looking appearance, it's best to replace a manufacturer's dedicated turnout and other controls with miniature switches. Several types can duplicate the functions of most control devices that come with train components.

You will need three types of switches to handle the various jobs required on a model railroad. They are commonly identified as SPST, SPDT, and DPDT. The letter P stands for pole, T for throw, S for single, and D for double. A *pole* is a point of electrical connection, and a *throw* identifies what happens when you move the switch handle. For example, the on/off switch shown in figure **4** is a single-pole single-throw (SPST) switch. This switch will accommodate just one electrical input, so it has a single pole. Since the function of the switch itself is either to allow or to interrupt the flow of current, it has just a single function, or throw.

Somewhat more versatile is the SPDT (single-pole double-throw) switch with three wire connection points, **11**. The center connection point is the pole, and the two outer ones represent the two throws. This type of switch is capable of performing two separate functions. There are two main types of SPDT switches—conventional and center-off. A conventional SPDT is always turned on, either to the left throw or to the right throw. However, the handle on the center-off variety has a middle position where no current flows in either direction and can therefore function as an on/off switch.

A specialized type of SPDT supplied with Atlas turnouts is a slide switch that moves the points of a turnout to either the straight or curved position, depending upon which way you slide it, **11**. This switch is always off in both left and right positions. To activate

11 Clockwise, from left, are several types of SPDT switches: a pair of automotive-type toggles, a pair of miniature toggles, and an Atlas turnout controller that combines a slide switch with a push button.

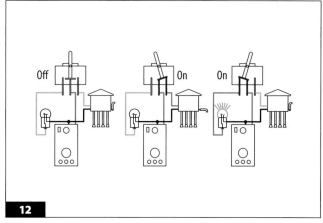

12 At left, no current passes through the switch. Move the handle to the left (center), and current goes to the right connection point. Move the handle to the right, and the left side of the switch is connected.

13 These automotive (left) and miniature (right) DPDT switches are shown in front and back views.

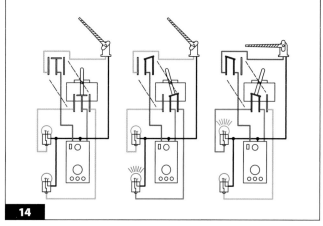

14 This wiring arrangement allows you to supply higher voltage to operate the gate and less voltage to give the bulbs longer life.

it, you first slide it to the desired side and then push in. (See Chapter 10 for more information about Atlas turnout controllers.)

When the handle of a center-off SPDT toggle switch is in the central position, no current passes through the switch, **12**. If you move the handle to the left, current is directed to the right-hand wire connection point. Move the handle to the right, and the left-hand side of the switch is connected. The single SPDT switch shown is being used to turn on a light and to lower the spout on a water tower, although it cannot do both at once. For that, you need a DPDT (double-pole double-throw) switch.

A DPDT is made up of two independent SPDT switches mounted side by side in a single case and operated by a single handle, **13**. There are six wire

connection points. The center two are the poles, and the outer ones represent the throws.

DPDTs are very versatile switches, capable of performing a variety of functions. They come in conventional and center-off versions, and the center-off type is more common and more useful. Figure **14** shows a DPDT with one set of contacts connected to the red and green bulbs of a block signal and the other set connected to a crossing gate. (The second set of connections for the gate is shown offset to the upper left of the toggle diagram.) In this example, two different accessory voltages are directed to the block signal (red wire) and the gate (blue wire).

Remember that one handle controls both sets of connections. At left in the figure, the switch is off. As shown in the center, when you throw the switch

to the left, power is routed to light the green bulb of the block signal, but no power reaches the gate. When you throw the switch right, power is directed to light the red bulb of the block signal, and, at the same time, to lower the crossing gate.

In the example of a water tower and a lightbulb wired to an SPDT switch (figure **12**), the operator can only operate either the bulb or the tower, but not both at once. However, by using a DPDT switch instead, you can have the lightbulb remain on when the spout is lowered, as shown in figure **15**.

In wiring diagrams, DPDT toggle switches are usually represented schematically by showing only the six wire connection points on the bottom. The top three circles are the three connection points for one side of the switch, with the pole in the middle flanked by

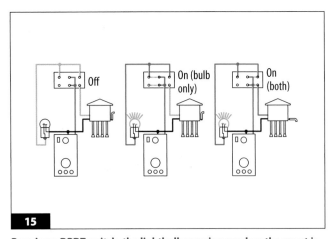

By using a DPDT switch, the lightbulb remains on when the spout is lowered.

Push buttons come in all sizes and several different types. The large and miniature push buttons with round, red tops are normally open models, as is the rectangular one at the bottom, a type supplied with Atlas uncouplers. The miniature black-topped one is a normally closed push button. The square-headed button operates like a toggle switch.

the two throw positions. The bottom three circles are the other side of the switch. The paths of electrical connection inside the switch are shown by dashed lines.

Note that the power wire (red) is attached to both center poles of the switch. This means that the same voltage will be applied to both sides. You can also provide different amounts of voltage for the water tower and the bulb, as shown with the block signal and crossing gate in figure **14**. (Other applications of these versatile DPDT switches are found in later chapters.)

Other switch types

A momentary contact switch (or spring return-to-center switch) is a variation found in both SPDT and DPDT

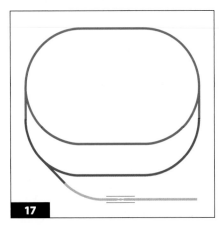

At each point where two colors meet, add an insulating pin in the middle rail to isolate the blocks.

switches. These specialized toggles are equipped with an internal spring that returns the handle to the off position automatically when released. In order to keep the circuit turned on, the operator must hold onto the handle. This type of switch is useful for operating turnouts, when just a brief application of current is required. These toggles often look just like the normal on/off variety, but when you move the handle to the side, it snaps back to the center position when released.

Another useful switch is the push button, and there are three common types for model railroad use, **16**. The most common type is the normally open button, which must be pushed to complete a circuit. This is the kind used to operate the water tower shown in photo **1**.

The normally closed variety always allows current to pass through until pushed. An example of a normally closed push button is the direction button on a transformer. This button interrupts the current to the track when pushed, causing the reverse unit in a locomotive to operate.

Normally open buttons and normally closed buttons are abbreviated NO and NC respectively. They are fitted with internal springs that return them to the original position when released. Some manufacturers color-code their push buttons—red for normally open and black for normally closed—but this is

not a universally applied standard. Be sure to read the packaging information when choosing the type you want.

The third type of push button operates like a toggle switch. When you press it to turn it on, it stays on until you press it again. Such buttons usually emit an audible click to indicate that they have functioned properly.

Graphic control panels

Miniature switches and push buttons are ideal for use on a graphic control panel. The first step in creating this type of panel is to make a diagram of the track plan, **17**. You can draw it freehand or use a computer drawing program such as AutoCAD or DesignCAD.

This simple layout design is divided into four blocks, represented by contrasting colors. Each point where two colors meet indicates a place where an insulating pin in the middle rail is needed to isolate the blocks. Unless the layout is very large, print the diagram on a single sheet of 8½ x 11 heavy paper, such as 65 lb. cover stock, available from office supply stores.

You can make the panel out of any relatively thin sheet of wood such as ⅛" or 3⁄16" plywood, but another option may save you a lot of time. Building supply stores stock pegboard with predrilled ¼" holes, **18**. The holes are the perfect size to accept miniature switches and push buttons, saving you

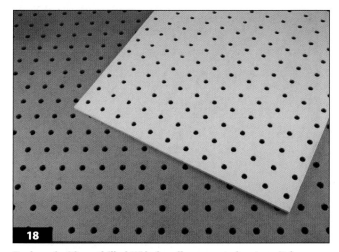

18

Pegboard with predrilled ¼" holes allows you to locate switches wherever needed.

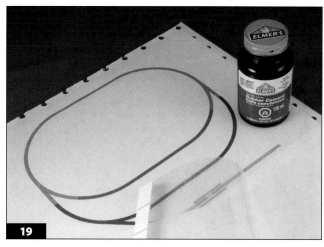

19

Clear plastic laminating sheets protect the surface of a control panel.

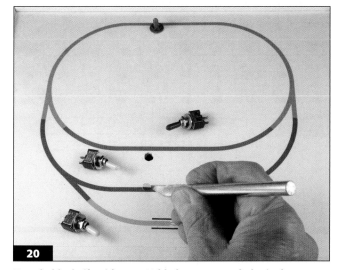

20

Use a hobby knife with a no. 11 blade to cut neat holes in the paper surface of the control panel.

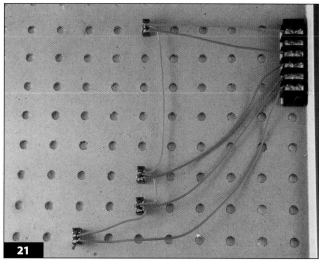

21

Barrier strips are the key to well-organized control panel wiring. Here, red jumper wires connect the central poles on the switches. The green wires connect the bottom pole of each switch to terminal screws on the barrier strip.

the chore of drilling holes for them. Cut a piece of pegboard large enough to accommodate the diagram. The panel in photo **18** measures 11¾" wide by 14" high, which leaves enough room at the bottom for adding extra switches to operate accessories. Pegboard comes either brown or preprimed in white. Whichever type you choose, I suggest that you give it two or three coats of white interior trim paint for a smooth surface.

When the paint is dry, fasten the track diagram to the painted side. Use a nonwater-based adhesive such as rubber cement. If your panel is larger than the diagram, also cover the remaining exposed pegboard with a second sheet

of paper, **19**. This area will accommodate switches and control boxes for accessories. To protect the surface, overlay the paper with self-adhesive plastic laminating sheets, which are available from office supply stores.

Edge the panel with your choice of molding for a neat appearance. I used simple L-shaped plastic molding, mitered at the corners and screwed to the panel. Hold the panel up to a strong light, so you can see where the holes are. Locate holes in the pegboard that are under or close to each of the colored track blocks in the drawing, **20**. Carefully cut out the paper with a narrow no. 11 blade in a hobby knife. Insert a 10-amp SPST

(on/off) miniature toggle switch into each of the holes from the back, and secure them in place with the washers and nuts that come with the switches. Install them so they will be turned on with the handle in the up position and off when they are down. This is easy to determine. Simply make sure that the outer connection point on the back of the switch is at the bottom.

Some miniature switches have fairly short collars and may not protrude far enough into the pegboard holes for the washers and nuts to fit over them. If so, shave the perimeter of the back of each hole with a hobby knife and no. 11 blade so the switches will fit. Pegboard is relatively soft and easy to carve.

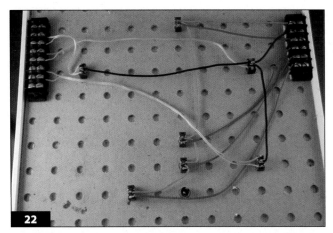

22

Use different terminal strips for different functions: track power at right and turnouts and uncouplers at left. The black ground wire runs from the second screw on the barrier strip to the central poles of the SPDT switches.

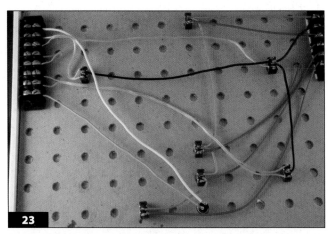

23

The speaker wires from the interior screws on the barrier strip provides connections to the turnouts. The white wire at the top of the barrier strip connects a push button at the lower right to the transformer, and the gray wire connects it to the uncoupler.

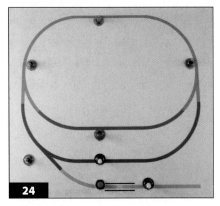

24

Color-code the handles on miniature toggle switches whenever possible for easy identification when operating the trains.

Organizing with barrier strips

The purpose of the SPST switches is to turn the track blocks on and off, and to accomplish this, they must be connected to the transformer in an efficient and economical manner. To avoid having too many wires attached directly to the transformer, let's install a barrier strip. Turn the panel over and, using double-faced tape, fasten a barrier strip near the edge of the pegboard.

Connect a single wire from the top terminal screw to the central pole of the nearest switch. Then run jumper wires from that pole to the central poles on all of the other switches, **21**. This becomes the main power wire connection from the transformer. Use 18 gauge wire for this application, as it is flexible and easy to work with and not too thick to attach to the small connection points on the

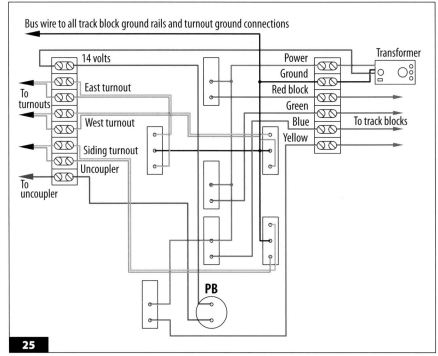

25

The wiring connections for the panel are arranged here to match their approximate positions in photos 22 and 23.

switches. Since all of these connections are relatively short, there is no danger of voltage drop. All of these wires should be permanently soldered to the toggle switches for positive electrical contact.

Skip the next terminal screw on the barrier strip, which will be used for the ground connection from the transformer. Connect wires from the bottom pole of each switch to separate terminal screws on the barrier strip. When you install the panel on the

layout, you will connect the power and ground wires from the transformer to the top two screws on the barrier strip. Then you will connect wires from the other four screws to the middle rails of the various track blocks, as described beginning on page 33. These wires should be a heavier gauge to prevent voltage drop, at least 16 and preferably 14 for large layouts.

Now locate holes that are over or close to each of the turnouts and install a miniature SPDT switch (the spring

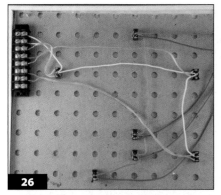

26

Use the minimum amount of wiring necessary to complete all connections. For the alternate wiring method shown in Figure 27 for Atlas or Z-Stuff turnout controllers, connect the middle poles of the SPDT switches to the top screw (accessory power screw) of the left-hand barrier strip.

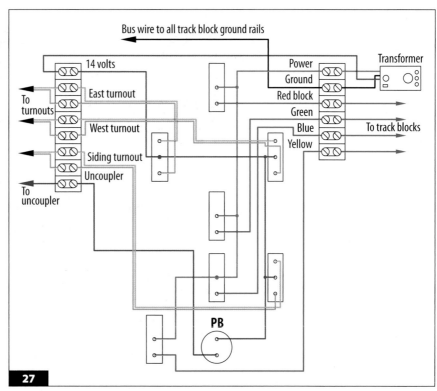

27

The dark blue accessory wire now connects to the central poles of the SPDT turnout switches instead of to the black ground wire. Otherwise, all the wiring remains the same.

return-to-center variety) at each location, **22**. These switches will replace the larger controllers supplied by the turnout manufacturers. Run a ground wire from the second screw on the barrier strip to the central poles of the SPDT switches. Momentary contact SPDT switches are sometimes hard to find. If so, simply use one side of the more commonly available momentary contact DPDTs.

Install an eight-position barrier strip on the opposite side of the panel. (Separating the two barrier strips spreads out the wiring and makes it appear less complex.) Connect wires from the two outer poles of each SPDT switch to screws on the barrier strip, starting with the second screw down from the top, **23**. These wires provide the connections to the turnouts themselves. Lightweight wire, 22 or 24 gauge, is adequate for low amperage circuits such as these. Audio speaker wire is a good and relatively inexpensive choice that comes in attached two-wire pairs.

Finally, if your uncoupler is a simple magnet, install a push button next to the symbol for it on the diagram. The top screw on the barrier strip is for accessory power from the transformer. Connect a wire from this top screw to one of the connection points on the push button. Connect another wire from the bottom screw on the barrier strip to the other connection

point on the push button. This screw is for the connection to the uncoupler itself. (These connections are shown in figures **23** and **27**.)

If you have an operating track section at that location instead of a simple magnet uncoupler, it is easier to use the dedicated control box supplied by the manufacturer. Position the box toward the bottom of the control panel. If you have several operating track sections on the layout, number the control boxes to match numbers written on the control panel. Wiring shortcuts for these track sections appear in Chapter 7.

To complete the graphic control panel, I added colored handle covers to the miniature toggle switches to match the track blocks for easy identification, **24**. No blue caps came with the switches, so I substituted white instead. The turnout switches have no colored caps to avoid any possible confusion with the block switches. This helps to avoid mistakes during operation.

The wiring connections for the panel are shown in figure **25**. The switches are represented graphically with their wire connection points. The push button is identified by the letters PB.

The colors match those shown in the photos, except for the white uncoupler power wire, which is dark blue, and the individual turnout wires, shown as pairs in orange and light blue. The transformer in this example is an Atlas model, with track power shown in red, accessory power in blue, and the ground in black.

Wiring premium turnouts

The method of wiring turnouts described works for all brands of turnouts and must be used with either Lionel FasTrack or MTH RealTrax turnouts. However, if you are using Atlas turnouts or the Z-Stuff controllers that come with Ross Custom Switches, there is an alternate method of wiring them that will save you some time and extra wiring. Instead of connecting the middle poles of the SPDT switches to ground, connect them instead to the accessory power screw of the second barrier strip, **26**. This eliminates the need for running a power wire directly to each turnout. More information about premium turnouts may be found in Chapter 10.

49

Figures **26** and **27** show an alternate wiring arrangement for use with Atlas or Z-Stuff turnout controllers. The colors match those shown in figure **25**.

Always try to use the fewest and shortest wires possible to keep the control panel uncluttered. Place labels next to the barrier strips to identify each wire connection, **28**. This is a great time-saver when you have to make changes or repairs. These labels eliminate the need to trace wires under a dark layout when something goes wrong—and something is bound to go wrong sometime. The screw marked power is from the throttle post of the transformer. The screw marked 14 volt is connected to an accessory post on the transformer. The other labels are self-explanatory.

The complexity apparent in these illustrations shows how vital it is to have careful organization of the wiring. For a relatively simple track plan like this one, with just seven toggles and a single push button, there are a great many wires needed to distribute the power properly. The number of wires expands almost exponentially as more track, turnouts, and uncouplers are added. For this reason, barrier terminal strips should be used for all connections and labeled carefully as to their function.

Large layout panels

For a large layout, one with a two-throttle transformer or even multiple transformers, organizing the wiring for the various circuits becomes even more critical. For example, both the MTH Z-4000 Transformer and the various editions of Lionel's ZW have eight wire posts on the back. Four of them are for ground and are connected together internally. Of the other four, two are for throttles and two are for accessories. Figure **29** shows how to connect a Z-4000 Transformer to a six-position barrier strip, from which all of the layout wiring is routed. Connections for a ZW Transformer are identical, although the two accessory posts provide variable voltage, instead of the 10- and 14-volt fixed voltages of the Z-4000.

The letter U has been used to designate the ground post on most

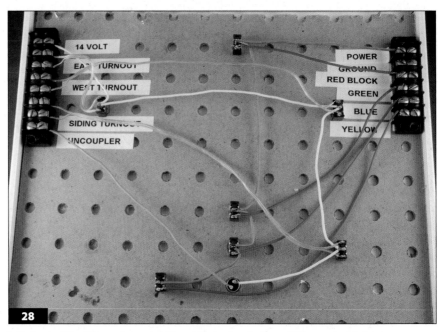

28

Label everything! Some day you will need to know what one of these wires is for.

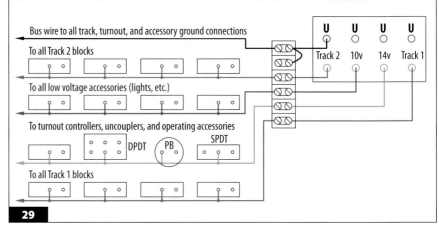

29

Four switches are connected to each circuit.

large transformers manufactured since World War II. Because a layout requires a large number of ground connections, two of the screws on the barrier strip are grounded. You could run two separate wires from the transformer to the barrier strip, but this is not necessary because all the ground posts on the transformer are connected internally. Instead, the two screws are connected together by a short jumper wire.

The ground posts on the Z-4000 Transformer have black caps, making them easy to identify. All of the power posts have red caps, but in figure **29**, the two track power circuits are shown in red and green to differentiate between them, and

the accessory posts are shown in two shades of blue.

Four switches are shown connected to each of the circuits, but on a large layout, many more would be required. For example, each turnout needs its own SPDT switch, and it's not uncommon to have a dozen or more turnouts on a layout. The same is true of uncouplers and accessories, and operating track sections each need a DPDT switch, one of which is shown in the 14-volt circuit.

There are minor differences between the turnouts and operating track sections made by major manufacturers, requiring slightly different wiring patterns, which are discussed in Chapter 7.

CHAPTER SEVEN

Wiring track components

For layout expansion, the four most important pieces of track are turnouts, uncouplers, operating track sections, and crossings, **1**. All of these items except crossings require wired connections, and all are easy to use with the controllers that the manufacturers package with them. However, there are strong reasons for employing alternate wiring patterns. For example, by substituting miniature toggle switches for bulky controllers, you can save valuable space on a control panel. Also, it is possible to reduce the amount of wiring that must be attached to each device, and on a large layout, the savings in time and money can be substantial.

The three largest train set manufacturers, Atlas O, MTH, and Lionel, make a variety of track components for expanding a layout. Examples of the four most common track pieces for expanding a layout are, clockwise from lower left, an MTH RealTrax crossing, a Lionel FasTrack remote control turnout, a Lionel FasTrack operating track section, and an Atlas O Industrial Rail uncoupler.

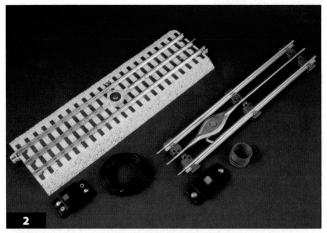

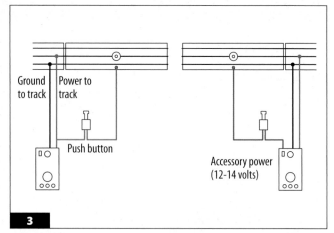

Atlas Industrial Rail (left) and Lionel traditional track uncouplers are fitted with central electromagnets. Lionel makes a similar unit for its FasTrack system, as well as one for use with traditional O-27 track (right).

Track power (left) is one way to operate an uncoupler magnet, but if a train is moving slowly, the low voltage may not open the couplers. Using fixed accessory voltage from the transformer (right) provides more consistent operation.

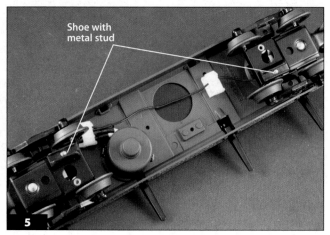

The magnet in an uncoupling track can also activate some operating cars, such as this Lionel 9228 boxcar.

Lionel inventors developed the sliding shoe method of getting electricity to an operating car to dump its load or open its couplers.

Basic uncoupling tracks

The most common type of uncoupling track consists of a simple electromagnet that interrupts the third rail, 2. Cars are equipped with a metallic thumbtack-like disk or a flat metal plate beneath each coupler assembly. When the magnet is energized, it pulls down on the disk or plate to open the coupler's jaws. These traditional uncoupling tracks work with the majority of O gauge rolling stock produced by various manufacturers. Manufacturers of premium track products make similar items (see Chapter 10).

Just a single power wire is required for installation. Because the magnet is grounded to the outside rails, you don't need a ground wire. Each uncoupler comes with a rectangular push button and a coil of hookup wire, or you can

substitute a miniature push button as described in Chapter 6.

There are two ways to connect the magnet, 3. The simplest method is to use track power, but this doesn't work well if a train is traveling slowly. In that case, the low voltage present in the track may not be sufficient to energize the magnet enough to open the couplers. Using fixed accessory voltage from the transformer provides more consistent and positive operation. An accessory voltage post provides about 12–14 volts to the magnet through a push button.

Some operating cars, such as the Lionel 9228 Canadian Pacific boxcar, work using the same magnetic principle, 4. A metal disk mounted on the underside is connected to a spring-loaded mechanism inside the car.

When the car passes over the magnet in the track, the disk is pulled down and a latch releases the door. A spring opens the door and moves the figure forward. It isn't necessary to stop the train to initiate this action. The magnet does its work as the car passes overhead if the train is not moving too rapidly.

Operating track sections

With the following announcement, Lionel's 1938 catalog introduced a novel piece of engineering that revolutionized the toy train industry: "Hey fellows—watch what happens now when you press a button. Magic remote controls start, stop, or reverse your Lionel—blow its realistic whistle—load and unload freight cars—actually couple and uncouple trains—electrically." Of course, direction control was more

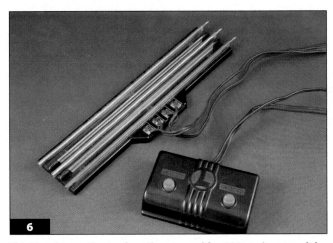

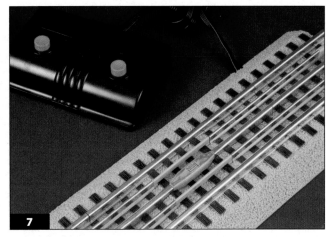

This Lionel operating track section came with a 1941 train set, and the principles behind it are still found in current operating track sections.

A Lionel FasTrack operating track section has the same style control box as the 1941 version. (If it ain't broke, don't fix it!)

than a decade old by that time, and onboard whistles had been around for a few years, but the really big news was remote control uncoupling and the first operating freight car, a modest little coal dumper.

The company had finally solved a problem that puzzled the industry for years—how to transfer power to couplers or to a dump mechanism without interfering with the electricity in the track that runs the trains. The solution was somewhat complex but very effective. Each freight or passenger car carried a small plastic shoe on each truck with a metal stud in the center, **5**. Each coupler was fitted with a solenoid, an electromagnetic device that generates action. The power wires of the couplers' solenoids were wired to the shoes and grounded to the car body. On the dump car, another solenoid that tilted the bin was wired to one shoe and grounded to the other.

To get power to the shoes, Lionel created a section of straight track fitted with two extra rails, mounted on either side of the middle rail, **6**. Four wires connected this track section to a plastic control box with two push buttons on it, one labeled *uncouple* and the other *unload*. Pushing the uncouple button sent track power to both auxiliary rails, which fired the grounded solenoids in the couplers and opened them when the car entered the track section. With the dump car stopped over this piece of track, pushing the unload button powered one auxiliary rail and grounded the other one, which activated the

dump mechanism solenoid and tilted the bin.

There were a few minor problems inherent in this system. There had to be power in the track for the operating section to work, so the locomotive pulling the train had to be fitted with a sequential reverse unit so it could stand in neutral while the car unloaded. Also, because the unload button sent power to one of the auxiliary rails, and thus to one of the couplers, that coupler opened whenever the car dumped its load. Operators soon compensated for the latter problem by backing up the train slightly until the coupler latched again.

That was over seven decades ago, and this clever five-rail operating track section is still the most common method for achieving remote control uncoupling and freight delivery on three-rail train layouts. The track sections look a bit more modern, but the principles involved are the same. Both Lionel and MTH market similar operating track sections for their various lines of track products, and variations on the idea are made by premium track manufacturers.

The Lionel FasTrack version is typical of these various products, **7**. In addition to the auxiliary rails, it also contains a small magnet in the center to uncouple cars with pull-down thumbtacks or metal plates. This is now the standard uncoupling mechanism for most of the industry. Changing to magnetic rather than electric uncoupling solved the problem of a coupler opening during freight

delivery. Lionel introduced this new system in 1948.

Although the mechanisms in operating cars have been refined and updated with new technology, the principle remains the same as in 1938. Pushing the unload button delivers the freight. Pushing the uncouple button energizes the magnet for uncoupling, and it also powers both auxiliary rails for those operators who still run vintage equipment with electric couplers.

Photo **8** shows an assortment of Lionel freight cars that communicate with an operating track section by means of sliding shoes on their trucks. On the upper track are a log dump car and a lumber unloader with two miniature workmen who appear to throw long boards to the ground, one at a time. On the lower track are an automatic milk car (Lionel's first car with an animated human figure), a coal dump car, and a barrel unloader.

Manufacturers have found other ways to utilize the operating track system. MTH makes an animated caboose with a lantern-carrying brakeman standing on the rear platform, **9**. This car contains a slow-geared motor that is turned on by the unload button of the control box. The lantern lights up red, and the figure sidles to the top of the steps and leans out far enough to see ahead along the track. It's fascinating to watch.

You can use an operating track section just as it comes from the manufacturer with the four wires that connect the track to the control box. In this

Operating cars give the trains a purpose such as the delivery of various kinds of freight.

Push a button and watch the brakeman signal to the engineer with his lantern.

case, it uses track power. There are a few disadvantages to this, however. The locomotive cannot be shut down but must stand in neutral while freight is delivered, although with today's modern reverse units, this isn't a serious problem. You must also adjust the voltage going to the track to the proper level to make the freight operation move at a realistic speed—again, not a major inconvenience. But if you use TMCC or DCS command control, there will be a full 18 volts of current in the track at all times, which is too much for most operating cars.

There are two persuasive reasons for wiring the operating track section directly to an accessory voltage post of the transformer rather than to track power. If you connect to the transformer, the operating cars will always receive the same level of voltage, regardless of what is happening with trains elsewhere on the layout. Secondly, these track sections are often located at a distance from the control panel, requiring you to splice extra wire in between the track and the control box.

The left diagram in figure 10 shows the connection to fixed or adjustable voltage posts for most operating track sections, including MTH RealTrax, Lionel FasTrack, and vintage Lionel O gauge track. Disconnect the power wire (shown in blue) from the track and attach it to the fixed or variable voltage post. The left wire is the ground wire. You can connect it to the transformer or to the ground bus wire anywhere on the layout.

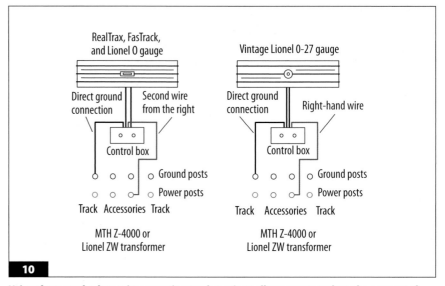

Using these methods to wire operating track sections allows you to reduce the amount of wire needed by almost half.

If you are using Lionel O-27 operating track sections from the late 1940s through the 1960s, use the wiring scheme shown in the right diagram of figure 10. The power wire is the one at the extreme right.

Choose an appropriate accessory post, such as the 14-volt post on an MTH Z-4000 Transformer. Most operating cars work well with this voltage, although there are exceptions. For example, 14 volts will make the little figure in most Lionel milk cars deliver the cans too quickly, usually knocking them over. On a Lionel ZW or Atlas transformer, you can adjust the accessory voltage to whatever level works best for each car. Milk cars perform well at about 11–12 volts.

Remote control turnouts

Like operating track sections, turnouts may be used without any modifications to the wiring. The only disadvantages are the very large size of their control boxes and the need to splice extra wire into the cables that connect the control boxes and the turnouts to each other when they are far from the control panel.

The control boxes for Lionel FasTrack turnouts, 11, and MTH RealTrax turnouts are easy to use, especially by children, but they take up an enormous amount of room on a control panel, especially if you have a large number of them. They are far too big to incorporate into a graphic control panel. You can substitute an SPDT toggle switch for the control box.

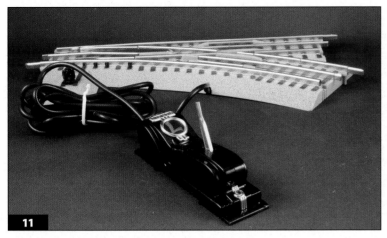

11

Turnout control boxes can overwhelm a control panel.

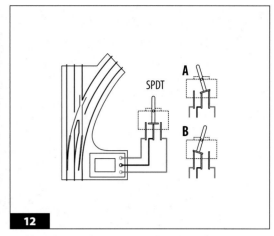

12

Pushing the switch to A moves the rails to the curved position and pushing it to B moves them straight.

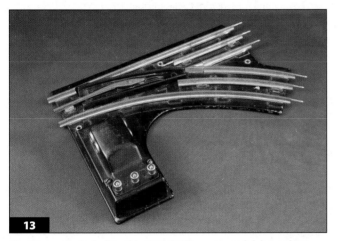

13

Most turnouts, including this 1941 O-27 gauge model, have three wire connection points.

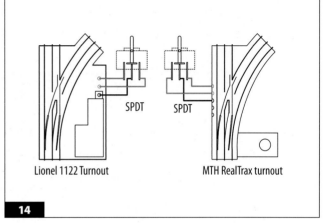

14

You can follow these diagrams to wire older Lionel and modern MTH turnouts.

Choose the momentary contact, or spring return-to-center, type of SPDT switch. The handles on these switches are fitted with internal springs. If you press them in either direction, they return to the center position when you release them. Current passes through them only when the handles are held down. When wired as shown in figure **12**, pressing the switch one way turns the rails to the straight position, and pressing the switch the other way turns the rails to the curved position. (See Chapter 6 for more about switches.)

Virtually all toy train turnouts are wired in the same way, with just three wires needed to make the rails move. Most draw power from the track, although some, like Lionel's 022 model introduced in the 1930s and the MTH RealTrax unit, can be attached to a fixed voltage post. There are

three binding posts on most of these turnouts, and with few exceptions, the middle post is the ground, and the two outer posts are for the straight and curved positions of the rails.

The Lionel pre-World War II 1121 Turnout in photo **13** is typical of this type. On this particular model, the left post is for the curved position and the right post is for straight. Connect these posts to the SPDT switch as shown in figure **12**. This diagram shows the internal connections of the SPDT switch. When you push the handle of the switch one way (A), a ground connection is made between the middle post and the left post (red), and the turnout moves to the curved position. When you move the switch the other way (B), the right post (green) is grounded.

Lionel's 1122 O-27 Turnouts, made from the late 1940s through the 1960s

(and produced ever since under different catalogue numbers), have the posts arranged slightly differently. The ground post is located next to the box that covers the mechanism and is mounted on a shiny rectangular metal plate for identification. The wiring pattern for these switches is shown at left in figure **14**.

At right in figure **14** is the wiring diagram for an MTH RealTrax turnout. Note that there are two additional posts on the MTH product where wires may be attached, **15**. These connections are for fixed voltage, and are explained fully in the instructions that come with each turnout.

Now let's save some wire. This will work with all of the turnouts described in this chapter as well as with most of the premium switch machines shown in Chapter 10. Instead of running all three wires from the control panel to

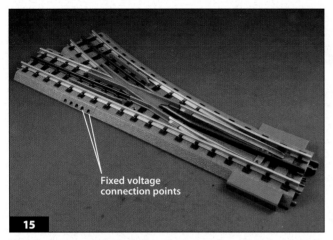

Fixed voltage connection points

15

MTH RealTrax turnouts have five wire connection points in the side of the roadbed. Two of these points are for fixed voltage and need not be used if the turnout draws its power from the track.

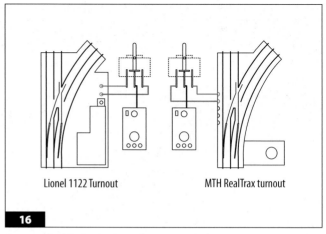

Lionel 1122 Turnout   MTH RealTrax turnout

16

Connect the black wire from the SPDT switch to a ground terminal on the transformer and run two wires from the SPDT switch, one for curved and one for straight, to the turnout.

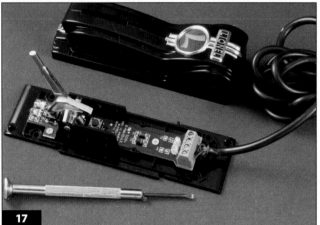

17

Lionel FasTrack control boxes look complicated inside, but you can replace them with simple SPDT switches.

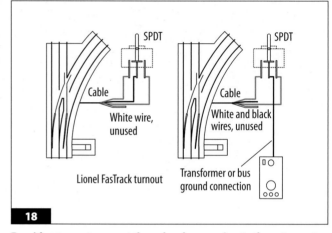

SPDT   SPDT

Cable   Cable

White wire, unused   White and black wires, unused

Lionel FasTrack turnout   Transformer or bus ground connection

18

For either turnout, connect the red and green wires to the outer posts of the switch.

the turnout, connect the black wire from the SPDT switch to a ground terminal on the transformer or the nearest ground bus wire, **16**. Now you will need to run only two wires from the SPDT switch instead of three, one for curved and one for straight. Since the toggle switch is close to the control panel and the transformer, you will have saved the long ground wire to the turnout.

To wire a Lionel FasTrack turnout to an SPDT toggle switch takes just a bit more work because the wires are all connected internally. Remove the four Phillips head screws from the bottom of the control box and open it up. Inside, you will find an electronics board with a green terminal block mounted on it, **17**. Make note of which color wires come from each of the four miniature screws on the terminal block in case you ever want to reconnect

the control box. Left to right they are green, black, red, and white.

Loosen the four screws in this block with a miniature screwdriver to release the four wires of the cable that comes from the turnout. These wires are color-coded: red for the curved position of the rails, green for straight, and black for ground. If you have to splice in extra wire to reach a distant turnout, use the same colors.

The white wire is not used when converting these turnouts to SPDT operation. Connect the black wire to the middle post of the SPDT switch. Connect the red and green wires to the outer posts of the switch, **18**.

You can also connect the black wire to the transformer ground or to the bus wire. However, because all the wires are enclosed in a cable, there will not be any savings unless you have to splice in

extra wire from a turnout that is some distance from the transformer. In that case, the black wire need not be spliced, as shown in the right diagram of the figure. Wrap both the white and black wire ends with a small piece of electrical tape to prevent them from coming in contact with any other wires.

The turnouts described in this chapter are excellent products, but sooner or later many serious model railroad enthusiasts may want to move up to a more realistic style of track, such as MTH ScaleTrax and those products made by Ross Custom Switches, GarGraves Trackage, and Atlas O. The wiring conventions used with these premium products are the subject of Chapter 10. But first we will explore the fascinating signals and crossing gates that fall under the category of trackside accessories in Chapter 8.

CHAPTER EIGHT

1

Automatic accessories

Automatic accessories respond to the presence of a train and include semaphores, block signals, and crossing gates, **1**. There are several methods for making them work. The oldest of them is the insulated track section, which dates all the way back to 1921, when Lionel introduced its first automatic accessory—the 69 and 069 Warning Signal. Close to a century later, the insulated track is still the most frequently used means of operating this type of trackside accessory. It is easy to wire and very dependable, but other methods offer certain advantages.

MTH crossing gates with warning flashers stand ready to protect motorists from the danger of passing trains.

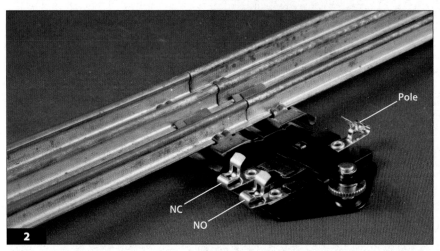

The Lionel 153C Contactor is a single-pole double-throw switch. It has clips for a normally open (NO) path, a normally closed (NC) path, and a pole that can be adjusted with a spring.

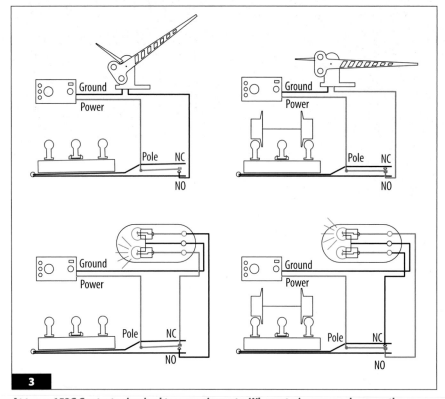

At top, a 153C Contactor is wired to a crossing gate. When a train presses down on the contactor, the pole moves to the NO contact, and the gate comes down. At bottom, the contactor is wired to a block signal.

The most recent development in accessory activation is the infrared sensor, which emits a beam of invisible light across the track. When a train passes by and breaks the beam, it activates an electronic circuit with the same function as an SPDT switch. MTH makes two versions, one for use with any make of track, and one designed to plug into its RealTrax system. Similar devices are made by Lionel and Z-Stuff for Trains.

Finally, the electronic relay is a device that has been used in model railroading for many years. It offers a positive method for operating all kinds of trackside accessories when used in conjunction with an insulated rail. These devices are available from any electronics supply store.

There are three main types of automatic trackside accessories: those with lights that either go on and off or that change color or position, those with action such as a crossing gate, and those that are lighted continuously and also have some form of action such as a semaphore. Action accessories are activated either by miniature motors or, especially vintage models, by a device called a *solenoid*. A solenoid resembles a spool with a hollow core and a coil of wire wrapped around it. When a current passes through the coil, it sets up a magnetic field that pushes a rod with enough pressure to activate an accessory.

The following sections of this chapter deal with different types of accessories and the activation methods appropriate to each.

Contactors

In 1936, Lionel introduced a new device designed to replace the insulated track section. The 41 Contactor was a pressure-operated SPST (on/off) switch with two Fahnestock clips for attaching wires. The contactor lay beneath the ties of a section of track and was spring-loaded to keep it open so that no electricity could pass through it until the weight of a passing train closed the circuit. That would activate any accessory wired to it. Spring tension was adjustable with a thumbscrew to fine-tune the operation.

One advantage of the contactor is that it can be moved to any part of a layout quickly and easily—just slide it out from under the ties. But contactors will not work on a permanent layout where the track is screwed to the table, because it must be free to move up and down as the train passes over. And while locomotives and heavy rolling stock can close the circuit, lightweight cars often lack enough mass to press the track down far enough to close the circuit.

The 41 Contactor was later joined with an SPDT (single-pole double-throw) model, 153C, **2**. This device has two paths that electrical current may take, one that remains closed when no train is present and one that closes when weight is applied. These two functions are usually referred to as normally closed (abbreviated NC) and normally open (NO). (Refer

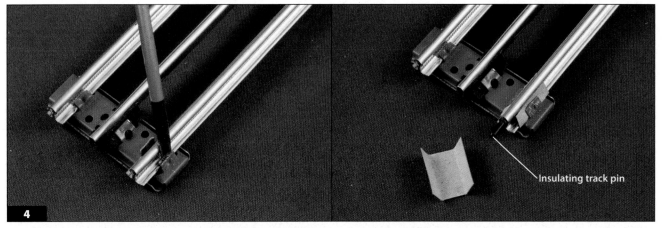

Pry up the clamps to free an outside track rail (left). Insulate the rail from all three ties with rectangles of thin cardstock (right), and place a plastic insulating track pin in both ends of the rail.

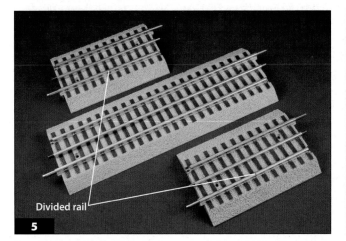

Lionel's Accessory Activator Pack creates an insulated track section approximately 15" long.

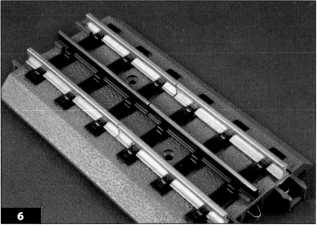

All three rails on this special MTH RealTrax section are insulated by gaps at the center.

to Chapter 6 for more information about SPDT and other types of switches.)

This contactor was originally designed to accompany the 153 Block Signal, and it lighted the green bulb until a train came near, after which the signal changed to red. Some Lionel accessories still come with a 153C Contactor, and MTH Electric Trains makes a similar mechanical device called a TAD (Track Activation Device). Today, these contactors are mostly used on temporary layouts.

Figure **3** is a schematic representation of how a 153C Contactor works with several accessories. At top, a vintage Lionel 152 Crossing Gate is wired to ground and to the contactor's NO clip. When no train is present, the adjustment spring in the contactor keeps the pole touching the NC contact, and no electricity reaches the gate.

When a train arrives and presses down on the contactor, the pole moves to the NO contact. This completes the circuit and sends power to the gate, which comes down to block model vehicular traffic.

With a three-wire 153 Block Signal (bottom), the ground wire is attached to the middle post, which grounds both of the lightbulbs. The NO contact is wired to the post for the green bulb, and when no train is present, the green bulb lights. When a train arrives, the pole moves away from the NC contact, turning off the green bulb, and moves to the NO contact to light the red bulb instead.

Insulated track sections

The word *insulated* in an insulated track section refers to the isolation of one of the outside rails from electrical contact with adjoining sections of

track. You can purchase ready-made insulated O-27 and O gauge traditional track sections from Lionel or make them yourself.

The two outside rails of traditional O-27 and O gauge toy train track are connected together electrically through the metal ties. In order to insulate one of the outer rails, you must remove the rail by prying up the metal clamps that hold it to the ties and insert some form of insulating material between the rail and all the ties in the section, **4**. You then insert insulated track pins in both ends of the rail.

Like traditional toy train track, Lionel FasTrack sections are constructed with both outside rails connected together electrically. It is difficult and time consuming to convert these sections to an insulated outside rail. Lionel sells them ready-made, however, in the 12029 Accessory Activator

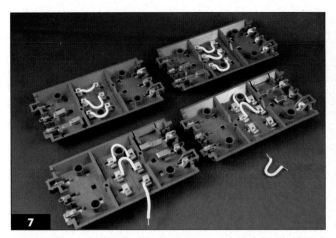

Jumper wires under the RealTrax base connect the insulated sides of the rails together. To make an insulated section, remove the jumper from one outside rail on both track sections.

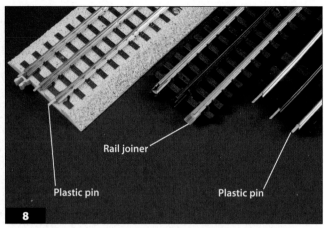

From left to right are track sections for Atlas Industrial Rail, Atlas 21st Century, and Ross Custom Switches. To make an insulated track section for the solid rails of Atlas 21st Century (center), use a fitted plastic rail joiner. For the other track sections, use plastic pins.

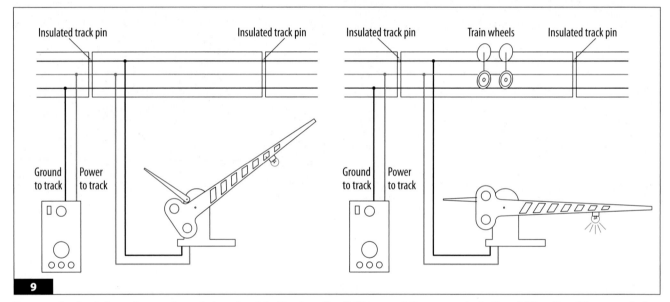

To connect a simple two-wire crossing gate to an insulated track section (left), connect the power wire to the middle rail and the ground wire to the insulated rail. At right, metal train wheels complete the circuit, which lights the bulb and lowers the gate.

Pack, **5**. You can also buy extra track sections for longer insulated rails with the 12027 Accessory Activation Extender.

The Accessory Activator Pack consists of a 10" section on which the two outside rails are not connected electrically. Each of the two shorter sections has one divided outside rail that prevents the passage of electricity. When you place a short section on either end of the long section, with the rail gaps on the same side, you create a 15" insulated section.

MTH RealTrax also creates an insulated track section from two half sections of track (40-1029), **6**. The rails of

each half section are interrupted in the center and insulated so that no current passes from one side of the track to the other. However, the rails are connected together by jumper wires on the underside to pass the current, **7**. To create an insulated track, disconnect the jumper wires from one outside rail on both sections of track.

The outside rails of MTH RealTrax sections are not connected together electrically. The outside rail of any regular track sections placed between these two halves will be insulated too. You don't need a special activation extender track like the one needed with Lionel FasTrack. (You can also insulate

the outside rails of any RealTrax section by bending the electrical contacts, as shown on page 28.)

All other track systems come with no electrical connection between the two outside rails. To insulate a rail from adjoining sections, place plastic track pins or rail joiners in both ends of the rail, **8**.

How insulated track sections work

Figure **9** shows how to connect a simple two-wire crossing gate (the vintage Lionel 152 model) to an insulated track section. The simplest method has the power wire going to the middle rail and the ground wire to the insulated rail. Notice that the ground connection from the transformer goes to the outside rail opposite the side where the insulated rail is located, while the ground connection from the gate goes to the insulated outside rail. The gate is not lowered because there is no ground connection to the gate.

In the right illustration, the wiring is exactly the same. The only difference is that a train has entered the insulated track section (symbolized by the pairs of wheels). Because the wheels and their axles are metal, an electrical connection is transferred from the grounded rail to the insulated rail, which completes the circuit to the gate and lowers it and lights the bulb.

You will want to have enough insulated track sections so that the gate will come down before the train reaches the grade crossing and stays down until the train has gone past. Any two-wire accessory may be connected to an insulated track section in this manner for automatic operation.

The crossing gate is a simple two-wire accessory, and it is either on when a train is present or off when the train has departed. Some three-wire accessories, such as Lionel's vintage 151 Semaphore or the more modern 22944 version, may also be connected to an insulated track section, **10**. The difference between these signals and the crossing gate is that the light in the semaphore remains on at all times. The semaphore arm lowers only when a train passes by. The wiring diagram is shown in figure **11**. (This diagram and

10

The passing train has activated this Lionel semaphore, dropping the arm and showing a red warning light.

those remaining in this chapter show the basic ground connections made to a bus wire that encircles the layout. This system of wiring is described fully in Chapter 4.)

In the left diagram, a Lionel 151 Semaphore, which has three screw-type posts on the base where wires are connected, has the accessory power wire (blue) connected between the middle post and the accessory voltage post of the transformer. The lower post is grounded to the bus wire, and whenever the transformer is on, the bulb in the semaphore lights, shining through the green lens in the arm. When a train enters the insulated track, the wire from the insulated rail carries the ground connection to the upper post,

and the internal solenoid lowers the arm. This brings the red lens in front of the bulb.

An optional but recommended on/off toggle switch is shown in the power wire. If you allow a train to remain standing on the insulated track, the semaphore arm will stay down and the solenoid will emit a buzzing sound. It may also overheat after awhile, so it is desirable to be able to turn it off.

The diagram on the right shows the Lionel 22944 Mainline Semaphore, which is connected to the transformer using color-coded wires that extend out from under the base. The power wire on this accessory is red and the ground wire is green—these two wires light the

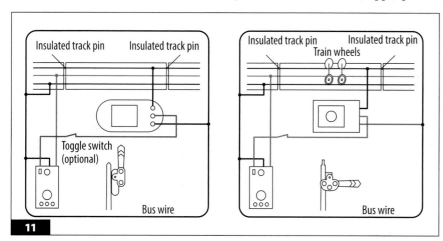

11

This figure shows how insulated track sections work with two types of semaphore signals, a vintage 151 (left) and a more modern 22944, both made by Lionel.

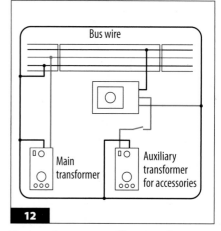

12

You can also use an auxiliary transformer to power accessories.

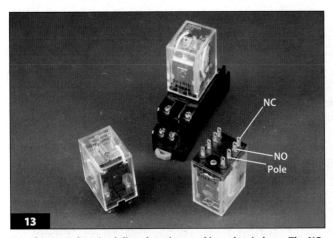

13

14

AC relays may be wired directly or inserted in a plug-in base. The NO, NC, and pole wiring connection points are shown.

With a bridge rectifier, you can use a DC relay to change the current to AC. To connect the rectifier to the relay, attach the + and – leads on the rectifier to the coil contacts on the relay.

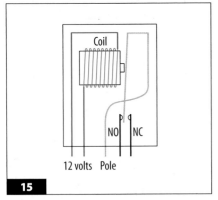

15

When 12 volts are applied to the coil, it becomes an electromagnet and attracts the rotating arm of the pole so that it moves away from contact NC and touches contact NO.

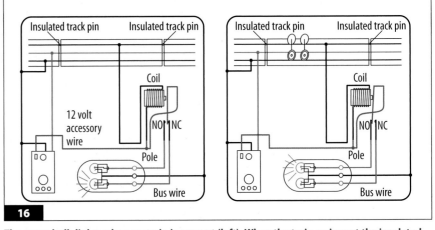

16

The green bulb lights when no train is present (left). When the train arrives at the insulated track, the wheels complete the ground connection to the coil of the relay coil. The relay magnet moves the pole to contact NO, which turns off the green bulb and lights the red one.

bulb. The white wire connects to the insulated rail to lower the arm when a train enters the insulated track. In this position, the bulb shines through the red lens. There is also an amber lens between the green and red lenses, but the arm does not stop in that position.

It is advisable to connect all lighted trackside accessories to an accessory post on the transformer, either fixed or variable voltage. This ensures that the light will remain at a constant brightness and not grow dimmer when the train slows down. In this example, the semaphore is connected to the variable voltage post of an Atlas transformer set to 10–12 volts. The power wire is attached to the center post, which is connected inside the semaphore to both the light bulb and the solenoid that lowers the arm.

You can also use an auxiliary transformer to power these accessories, provided both transformers are grounded to the bus wire and are in phase, **12**. (See Chapter 9 for further information about using auxiliary transformers for accessories.)

Electronic relays

Semaphores and crossing gates have only one operation—they are either on, with the gate or the semaphore arm lowered, or off, depending upon whether a train is present. The lightbulb in the semaphore is on continuously. By contrast, a block signal such as Lionel's vintage 153 has two bulbs (red and green) that light alternately, depending upon whether a train is present. To make it work properly, you need a way to turn one bulb off when the other one is on.

The 153 Block Signal was sold with a 153C under-the-track contactor. When no train was near, the spring in the contactor kept the circuit to the green bulb closed. But when a train pressed down on the track, it opened the green bulb circuit and closed the one connected to the red bulb, so the signal changed from green to red, **3**. This only works on a temporary layout, where the track is not screwed to the table.

On a permanent layout, where the track is fastened down, there are two substitutes for the contactor: an infrared sensor, explained on page 64, and a miniature electronic relay, **13**.

An electronic relay is simply a type of switch, but instead of being thrown by hand, it is operated by a magnetic coil. Most miniature relays are double-pole double-throw (DPDT) types,

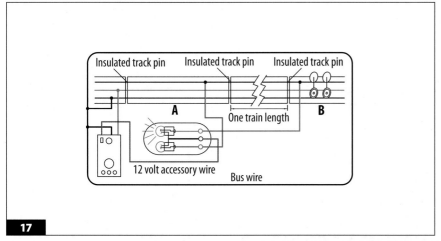

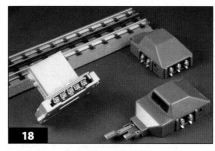

18 MTH infrared detectors (ITAD) are solid-state replacements for traditional electronic relays. The ScaleTrax model looks like a relay case. Here, it is tilted back to show the wire connection points under a flip-up panel. One RealTrax model is shown plugged into a track section, and another is detached to show the connectors that insert into the track.

17 When a train enters track A, the wheels complete the ground connection to light the signal's green bulb. When the train reaches section B, the red light comes on.

19 From left to right, this MTH signal indicates that there is no train in the block (vertical position), a train is present (horizontal position), and a train is leaving the area (diagonal position).

which are the same as two single-pole double-throw (SPDT) switches mounted side by side. You can buy them for either direct current (DC) or alternating current (AC) applications. You will need an AC relay to work with the AC transformers that operate O gauge trains. They come in various voltage ranges, and the 12-volt size is best, as it operates well within a range of 8–18 volts from the accessory post of a transformer. If you can't locate a 12-volt AC relay, a 24-volt relay will also work, provided it is powered by at least 14 volts. These relays have a wide tolerance for power input.

DC relays
It is often easier to find direct current (DC) relays than the somewhat less common alternating current (AC) variety. A DC relay will not work with

an AC transformer, but you can convert the current with a small bridge rectifier, available from electronics supply stores, **14**. Four stiff wire leads emerge from the molded case of the rectifier, labeled + (plus), – (minus), and AC. Attach the + and – leads to the coil contacts on the relay. It doesn't matter which way they are connected. Connect the AC leads to the transformer's accessory power and to whatever mechanism you are using to activate the relay, such as an insulated outside rail.

Using relays
Figure **15** shows the parts of an electronic relay: the electromagnetic coil, the pole with its movable arm, and two contacts (open and closed). The coil is wrapped with very thin wire (shown in green). The pole (orange) includes a

rotating arm that moves back and forth between the NO and NC contacts. Contact NC allows current from the pole to pass through it when the coil is not operating. Contact NO has no current passing through it when the coil is not operating.

When 12 volts are applied to the coil, the coil becomes an electromagnet and attracts the rotating arm of the pole so that it moves away from contact NC and touches contact NO.

We may connect this relay to any three-wire block signal that does not have built-in infrared detectors, such as a Lionel 153 Block Signal, **16**, or those made by MTH Electric Trains and NJ International (njinternational. com). To make the relay coil turn on when a train is present, connect one of the coil terminals to the accessory voltage post of the transformer and connect

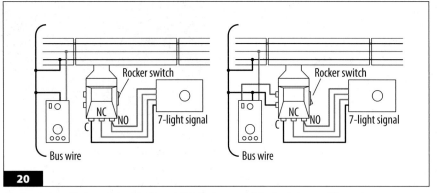

20

The basic installation of the RealTrax ITAD is shown at left. At right, you'll see the correct connections to an accessory voltage post.

21

When positioning this infrared detector from Z-Stuff for Trains, the sensor windows must face the track in order to detect a passing train.

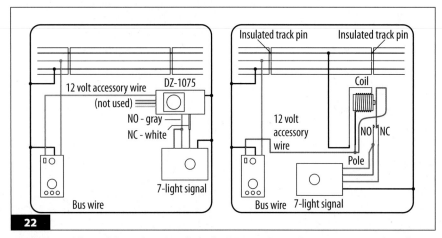

22

You only need four of the seven wires from the DZ-1075 Power Sensor to connect it to the MTH signal (left), or use an electronic relay to operate MTH signals (right).

the other coil terminal to the insulated rail. Also connect the accessory voltage to the pole of the relay. Connect contact NC to the green bulb of the block signal, and contact NO to the red bulb. The green bulb lights when no train is present. But when the train arrives at the insulated track, the wheels complete the ground connection to the coil of the relay. The relay magnet turns on and moves the pole to contact NO instead of NC, which turns off the green bulb and lights the red one.

You can also wire a block signal to two insulated track sections, and you won't need a relay at all. In fact, this method is closer to the way many prototype railroads use their signals, which is to have them turned off completely when there are no trains in the area and come on only when a train approaches, **17**. Position the two insulated track sections (A and B) at least one full train length apart. Assume that the train is traveling from left to right. When it enters track section A, the wheels complete the ground connection to light the green bulb, indicating clear track ahead. When the train reaches section B, the red light comes on instead to warn any following trains that the block ahead is occupied.

Infrared detectors

An infrared detector is an electronic relay known as an Infrared Track Activation Device (ITAD) that eliminates the need for an insulated section of track. MTH makes two versions of this device, **18**, and Lionel's IR53 Controller is similar. An infrared sensor works in the same manner as an electronic relay by providing both normally closed and normally open contacts, but instead of a magnetic coil and moving pole, it uses a solid-state circuit that is activated whenever a passing train interrupts a beam of light that shines across the track from the red plastic window in the ITAD.

The MTH RailKing 7-Light Block Signal provides information to approaching trains by the position of a row of three illuminated lights: horizontal, diagonal, or vertical, **19**. An electronic timing circuit inside the

This double-track position light signal from MTH represents a style of overhead bridge seen along the Pennsylvania Railroad right-of-way.

MTH trackside signals operate electronically and accept a wide range of accessory voltage input from any AC transformer.

signal controls the pattern changes. The lights are vertical when no train is present. When a train approaches, the signal moves to horizontal and stays there until the train leaves, after which the pattern changes to diagonal for about 10 seconds before returning to vertical. This signal is an excellent choice for operating with an ITAD.

The ITAD can draw its power from the track or from an auxiliary power supply. Remember that the outside rails of a RealTrax track section are not connected together. When using track power, make sure that the ITAD is inserted into the same side of the track as the ground connection from the transformer.

Basic installation is very simple. There are three screws at the back of the RealTrax ITAD for wire connections, from left to right: common (C, ground), NC, and NO. You need to connect four wires from the block signal to the ITAD, **20**. In the left illustration, you'll see red and blue wires going to the NO screw, green to the NC screw, and black to the common. The blue wire controls the auxiliary light below the main signal, and if wired to the NC connection instead, the auxiliary light will be on at all times except when a train is present. (It is shown lit at center in photo **19**.)

The RealTrax ITAD also has two screws for auxiliary power. The right illustration shows the correct connections to an accessory voltage post. A rocker switch on the right side of the

RealTrax ITAD must be moved to the Aux Power position.

The ScaleTrax ITAD has the same wire connection points (common, NC, and NO) hidden under a flip-up panel in the base. Because it is not attached to the track, two screws for power must be used. To operate properly, this ITAD must be located adjacent to the track, no farther than 1½" away, with the red sensor windows facing the track so that a passing train will break the beam of light.

MTH ITADs have sensitivity adjustments to adapt the sensor to different light and distance conditions. MTH provides instructions with all of its trackside accessories to show how to connect them to these infrared sensors.

You can also use an infrared detector, such as the DZ-1075 Trackside Power Sensor, next to the base of the 7-light signal, **21**. This unit is made by Z-Stuff for Trains and will operate any automatic accessory made by any manufacturer. It should be placed with the two sensor windows pointed across the track, no more than 1½" from the nearest rail. When a train passes by, it breaks the infrared beam and activates the connected accessory. Sensitivity adjustment screws can fine-tune the operation.

While seven wires emerge from the base of the DZ-1075 Power Sensor, you need only four to connect it to the MTH signal, **22**. The red wire connects to accessory power from the transformer, and the black wire is grounded to the bus wire. Connect the

white wire (NC) to the green wire of the MTH signal, and the gray wire (NO) to both the red and blue wires of the signal.

The green, blue, and yellow wires of the DZ-1075 provide options for more complex operation. Some are explained on page 66. Other options are beyond the scope of this book and are explained on the Z-Stuff for Trains website (z-stuff.net).

Finally, you can also use an electronic relay to operate MTH signals, **22**. The wiring is essentially the same as for the three-wire signals shown in figure **16**, except that two of the four wires from the signal (blue and red) are connected to the NO contact of the relay.

MTH also mounts a pair of position light signals on a model of a Pennsylvania Railroad two-track signal bridge, **23**. Each signal head has a separate set of three wires: black for common (ground), red for NO, and green for NC. It may be wired to an ITAD, a mechanical track detection device such as a 153C Contactor, a DPDT relay, or a Z-Stuff DZ-1075 Trackside Power Sensor, as shown in previous figures.

Both signal heads face the same direction. However, the accessory is fitted with two extra sets of wires that are internally connected to a pair of plug-in sockets on the opposite side of the bridge. Extra signal heads are available if you want to provide signal information for your trains traveling in either direction. Each head may

25 Z-Stuff for Trains semaphores (left) and block signals (right) have infrared detectors mounted in the base. These accessories are independent of the track and should be 1½" or closer to the nearest rail for proper operation.

27 This Atlas 21st Century signal comes with an industrial-style structure that holds the electronic components (the gray unit at left).

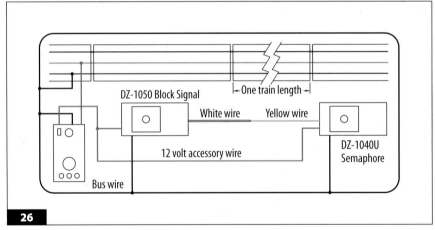

26 To keep the amber caution light on longer, connect the white wire of one signal to the yellow wire of another signal that is farther up the track.

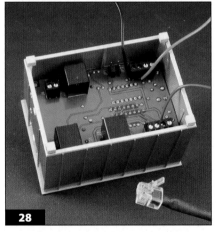

28 Atlas 21st Century circuit boards connect to the signals with a telephone-style plug.

be connected to a separate detection device, or two or more signals may be wired to the same device. Using separate detectors allows for prototypical signaling patterns.

An internal electronic circuit in MTH's 30-11036 3-light block signal controls its operation automatically, **24**. As with the Pennsylvania signal bridge, only three wire connections are necessary: black (common), red (NO), and green (NC). The signal normally shows green, and it turns red when a train approaches. Once the train has left the detection area, the signal changes to amber for about 10 seconds before returning to green.

Z-Stuff infrared signals

In addition to the DZ-1075 Trackside Power Sensor, Z-Stuff also manufactures various signals with infrared sensors built into the bases, such as the DZ-1040U Upper Quadrant Semaphore and DZ-1050 Block Signal, **25**. These accessories are completely independent of the track, and they should be located no more than 1½" from the nearest rail so that a passing train will interrupt the beam from the sensor.

Four wires extend from the base, but you only need two for basic installation: red for power and black for ground. The electronic circuitry inside

each signal controls the operation. The block signal normally shows a green light, but when a train breaks the sensor beam, it turns from green to red. Four seconds after the train leaves, it changes to amber for several seconds and then back to green. The semaphore operates the same way, with the addition of an arm that drops to the horizontal position when green changes to red, rises to a diagonal position on amber, and returns to vertical for green again.

The optional white and yellow wires provide for more sophisticated operation, **26**. For example, you may want to have the amber caution light remain

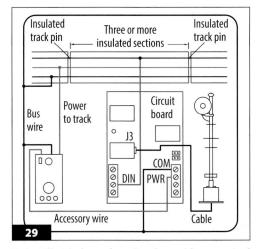

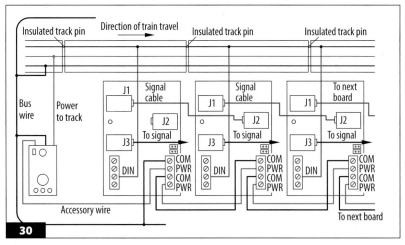

To install an independent signal, provide power (red wire) and ground (black wire) to the circuit board.

To link two or more signals together, install common (black) and power (red) wires between the circuit boards.

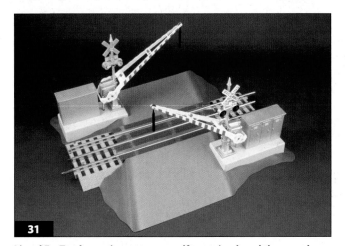

Lionel FasTrack crossing gates are self-contained, and they need no external wiring in order to operate.

MTH crossing gates are motorized for slow-motion action. The red lights in the warning flashers alternate in a realistic fashion.

on for a longer time after the train has passed by. To accomplish this, you can connect the white wire of one signal to the yellow wire of another signal farther up the track. This holds the up-track signal on amber until the down-track signal cycles. (For other advanced options, visit z-stuff.net.)

For independent operation of any two or more signals, connect the wires as shown in figure **26** but omit the white-to-yellow connection.

Atlas 21st Century Signal System
One of the most complex signaling devices available to O gauge railroaders, both three-rail and two-rail, is the 21st Century Signal System made by Atlas O, **27**. The one-light version shown here may be purchased separately or packaged in a set of four, each fitted with a single three-color LED

and a timing circuit that changes the light between green, amber, and red in prototypical sequence. The company also makes three-light signals, position light signals (similar to but smaller than the MTH 7-light signal), and dwarf signals.

The signals come packaged with rectangular enclosures that house circuit boards to control the lights, **28**. The signal connects to the circuit board by means of a telephone-style, plug-in cable. These units add authenticity when placed in an industrial scene, and in rural settings, they may be mounted underneath the layout.

Each signal may stand alone, controlled by an insulated track section. Two or more may also be located at intervals along the main line and wired together to operate in a realistic sequence as a train progresses. They

may be configured to light at all times or remain off until a train approaches, simulating one common prototype practice. Other options, which go beyond the scope of this book, include connecting the signals to turnouts and varying the time that the amber light remains on.

To install one independent signal, you must provide power (red) and ground (black) to the circuit board, **29**. The wires connect to miniature terminal blocks and are held in place by tiny screws. A third wire (green) connects an insulated track section to the Detector Input (labeled DIN). Atlas recommends that three or more adjacent 10" sections of track be insulated to keep the signal showing red for a realistic length of time.

Use an accessory post on the transformer to provide power. These signals

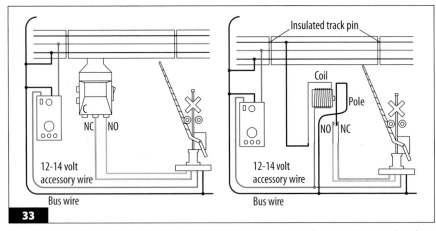

33

To connect crossing gates to a RealTrax ITAD (left), connect the red wire to 12–14 volts of accessory power, ground the black wire to the bus wire, connect the white wire to the NC post, and affix the yellow wire to the NO post. The connections for an electronic relay are similar (right).

accept a very wide range of voltage (6–22), so a post providing 12–14 volts is ideal. Ground the board to the nearest bus wire. Plug the cable from the signal into Jack 3 (J3). The signal changes from green to red when a train enters the insulated track, to amber when the train leaves the insulated track, and finally back to green after about 8 seconds.

To link two or more signals together, install common and power wires between the circuit boards, **30**. You can also connect each circuit board directly to the power and bus wires if that is more convenient. Plug one end of a signal cable into Jack 1 (J1) on the first board and the other end into Jack 2 (J2) on the second board. Continue to connect the boards together as shown in

blue on the diagram. These cables are available separately, and come in various lengths (7, 15, and 25 feet), depending upon how far apart your signals are. Additional options for more complex operation are provided in the instruction booklet that comes with each signal.

Crossing gates

Just one year after Lionel's first operating accessory appeared in 1922 (the 69 and 069 Warning Signal), the company introduced its first action accessory, the hugely oversized 077 Crossing Gate. Crossing gates have been available ever since from a variety of manufacturers, and today, many of these models are accurately scaled for O gauge and contain miniature motors that lower the gate arm at a realistically slow pace.

They can feature clanging bells and combine the gates with flashing warning lights, such as Lionel's FasTrack model, **31**.

The FasTrack gates are fully integrated into a section of track with a grade crossing molded into the roadbed. Also included are two short insulated track sections that connect to either end of the grade crossing. No wiring is required. The gates lower and the lights flash whenever a train's wheels enter the insulated section. The bell is very loud, but there is a switch to turn it off without affecting the action of the gates or the flashing lights.

The only problem with this system is that although the gates come down fairly quickly, the train will already be entering the grade crossing when they begin to move. To be realistic, they should come down well in advance to stop vehicular traffic. You can remedy this difficulty, however, by adding extra insulated sections (12027 Accessory Activator Extension) on either side of the crossing to increase the lead time for the gates to operate.

The motorized crossing gates made by MTH (30-11012) are designed to be operated by the company's track activation devices (ITAD), **32**. However, they may also be used with any brand of track in conjunction with either an infrared detector made by another manufacturer, such as the Z-Stuff for Trains DZ-1075, or an electronic relay. They will also work with an under-the-track mechanical contactor.

34

Z-Stuff for Trains crossing gates operate by optical detectors or with an insulated rail.

35

This Z-Stuff for Trains dwarf block signal contains an infrared detector, activated by the sensor window that faces the track.

To connect the crossing gates to a RealTrax ITAD, first connect the gate's red wire to 12–14 volts of accessory power and ground the black wire to the bus wire, **33**. Then connect the white wire to the NC post of the ITAD and the yellow wire to the NO post. (The blue wire is not used unless the gates are connected to an under-the-track mechanical contactor, such as an MTH TAD.)

The connections for an electronic relay are similar: red to power, black to ground, white to NC, and yellow to NO, **33**. Also connect the pole of the relay to the ground. The blue wire is needed when using a mechanical TAD (contactor) and is not used in this application. The gates can be wired to come down well in advance of an approaching train, depending upon how many insulated track sections you use.

Z-Stuff for Trains also makes a set of scale-sized motorized crossing gates (DZ-1010) with bell sounds and flashing warning lights, **34**. The relatively long arms on these gates make them ideal for wide grade crossings. They come packaged with two DZ-1011 Block Signal Detectors, **35**. These infrared detectors, which resemble prototype dwarf signals with operating red and green lights, should be placed far enough from the grade crossing to cause the gates to come down well in advance of an approaching train.

The two Z-Stuff gates are not identical. One has a raised industrial-style enclosure that conceals the electronics, while the other contains a small sensor mounted on its platform. The enclosure emits a beam of infrared light at an angle toward a sensor on the other gate's base. The gates must be no farther apart than 14" to allow proper operation as controlled by the beam of light, **36**. This generous distance should be enough to accommodate any reasonable width of roadway on a model railroad.

The block signal detectors should be mounted about a ½" from the track, with the sensor windows pointing across the rails. Although they are shown close to the gates in the diagram, they should be located at some

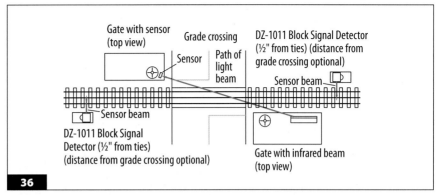

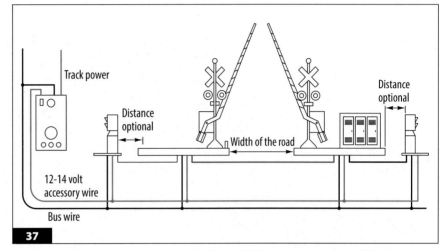

Note that there are no wires connected to the track. The optical sensors do all the work.

distance down the track so that the gates will come down well in advance of the approaching train.

When wired according to figure **37**, the gates start to come down when a train passes the first detector and stay down until the train has gone beyond the second detector.

You can adjust the gates to control the speed at which they operate (fast, medium, or slow). On the bottom of one gate, a very small panel contains four micro-miniature switches labeled SW1, SW2, SW3, and SW4. The gates will operate slowly if both SW3 and SW4 are closed, and operate quickly if they are both open. For medium speed, SW3 should be open and SW4 should be closed. You will need a very small flat-bladed screwdriver or a thin metal probe to push these tiny switches back and forth.

The only somewhat unrealistic feature of these gates—and it's a minor one shared with other gates—is that

with the infrared detectors located some distance from both sides of the grade crossing, the gates stay down until the train has passed by them both. On a prototype railroad, the gates rise as soon as a train clears the crossing. If the trains on your layout always travel in the same direction, you can use just one detector on the approach side of the crossing and eliminate the other one. Then the gates will come down in advance of the train's approach and rise as soon as the last car clears the crossing.

You can also use these gates on a double-track crossing, and if the direction of travel on each track is always the same (for example, east to west on the right-hand track and west to east on the left-hand track), you need only one detector for each line on the approach side of the crossing. But if trains may travel in either direction on both tracks, you need two more DZ-1011 detectors to make them work.

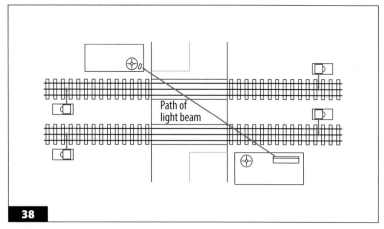

38

This diagram shows how to place four detectors at a double-track crossing where trains on either track may travel in either direction.

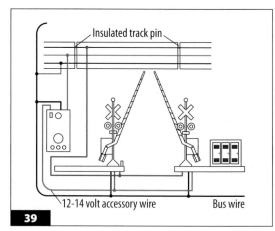

39

When wiring the gates to an insulated track, you only need to use three of each gate's wires.

40

This MTH grade crossing signal contains an electronic circuit that flashes the red lights alternately at a realistic speed.

41

The substantial speaker (center) that comes with these MTH warning flashers can be screwed to the underside of a layout in the vicinity of the grade crossing.

The infrared beams that these units emit only reach as far as a train passing on an adjacent track. Figure **38** shows the location of four detectors at a double-track crossing where trains on either track may travel in either direction.

These Z-Stuff crossing gates will also work with an insulated track section, in which case the DZ-1011 detectors are not used. Before installation, you must change the micro-miniature switch SW2 on the bottom of one gate to the open position. Then wire the gates as shown in figure **39**. Only three of each gate's wires are used.

The DZ-1011 Block Signal Detector is a versatile accessory, and when used alone, it functions as a dwarf signal, turning from green to red when a train passes by. It can also be wired to control other acces-

sories with the addition of a Z-Stuff DZ-1008 relay module. Wiring diagrams for all Z-Stuff products are found at z-stuff.net.

Flashing warning signals

Alternately flashing grade crossing signals are perhaps the most familiar piece of trackside equipment, and modern technology makes them very easy to connect. There are only two wires on most of them, such as the modern signal made by MTH (30-11006), **40**. The red wire receives 12–14 volts from the transformer, and the black wire is connected to an insulated track section.

The MTH 30-11014 grade crossing signal has an added bonus—a circuit that sends the sound of a ringing bell to a substantial speaker mounted under the layout, **41**. This accessory consists

of two signals, one for each side of a grade crossing, with the circuitry mounted in the bases.

If you are using an insulated track section to operate this accessory, connect the red wires from the two signals and the speaker to 12–14 volts of accessory power. Connect the black wires to the insulated rail.

You can also connect either of these grade crossing signals to any track detection device, including infrared sensors, ITADs, under-the-track contactors such as Lionel's 153C, and electronic relays. Use the normally open contact, and the lights will flash only when a train is approaching.

All the accessories described in this chapter are triggered automatically by trains. The next chapter deals with accessories that an operator controls independently.

CHAPTER NINE

1

Operating accessories

Almost from the earliest days of toy train manufacture, companies understood the desirability of placing their products in the context of the real world. A toy train running on a bare loop of track is fun, but the fascination wears off quickly unless there is some way to stimulate one's imagination and maintain interest. And so, instead of merely promoting the trains themselves, they set out to create a setting in which the toys could become the centerpiece of a miniature world. The concept of the toy train accessory was born, **1**. Among the first accessories to appear were elaborate tin stations and manually operated signals.

Lionel recently reproduced this American Flyer log loader, which originally appeared in the 1950s. Accessories that load and unload freight have always been popular. Lionel and American Flyer produced many such accessories during the 20th century.

2

Lots of lights look great in a dark room, but they put a heavy drain on the transformer's capacity. A large layout can have hundreds of lights.

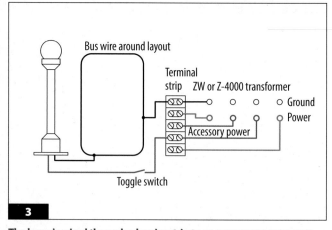

3

The lamp is wired through a barrier strip to an accessory power post (blue) and the bus wire ground connection.

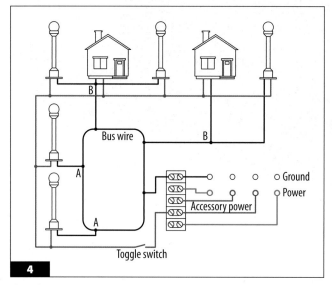

4

If you have several lampposts and buildings with lightbulbs inside, you can connect them all to one power wire.

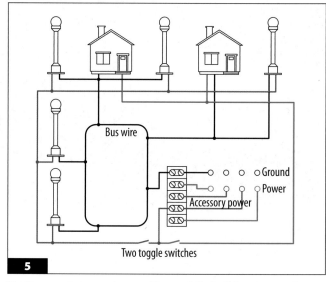

5

The lamppost power wires are blue, and the building power wires are green. Note that the ground connections are unchanged.

During the 1920s, Lionel produced not only stations and signals but miniature houses to create model villages, along with tunnels, bridges, and lampposts. Automatic accessories appeared at the same time. The first was a simple trackside warning signal with a bell that rang whenever a train passed by. This was quickly followed by automatic crossing gates, block signals, and an assortment of railroad structures such as signal towers, power houses, and water towers.

Until 1938, toy train accessories were either static—buildings, lampposts, and tunnels—or automatic trackside units such as gates and signals that operated in response to trains passing by. But in that late Depression year, Lionel introduced the first accessory that was controlled not by the trains but by the young engineers who owned them—the electric coal elevator. This accessory featured an endless chain fitted with miniature buckets that could hoist imitation coal up into an overhead bunker, store it, and then send it cascading into a waiting freight car, all at the touch of a button.

Lionel followed the coal elevator with three more impressive operating accessories: a log loader, a magnetic crane, and an electric bascule bridge that automatically stopped an approaching train as it began to lift.

The late 1940s and '50s welcomed an ever-increasing array of operating accessories to load and deliver various kinds of freight (coal, logs, barrels, scrap metal, and even culverts). They pumped oil, sawed logs into lumber, and fired missiles.

Today, we can buy more types of these fascinating toys than ever to fill even the most extensive model railroad.

All these accessories come with instructions for their use, and you can't go wrong by following the manufacturers' guidelines. However, there are tips and shortcuts that will make wiring easier and more economical to install, making these toys even more fun to use.

Basic principles

Whenever you add an accessory to a layout, you increase the electrical power requirement imposed upon the transformer. Depending upon the type of accessory, this extra load can be either negligible or considerable. The following principles should govern how you wire these toys.

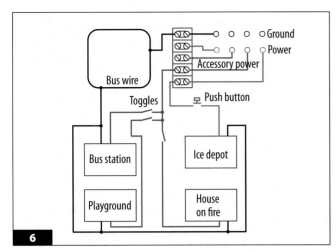

6

To operate these accessories independently, you will need a separate power wire and switch (or push button) for each one.

7

Two-wire accessories such as this Lionel Ice Depot need only a toggle switch or push button to operate them.

Use a second transformer. If you have a large number of accessories, especially lighted ones, use a second transformer solely for accessories. Large modern transformers, specifically the Lionel ZW and MTH Z-4000, are powerful and efficient, capable of handling multiple trains and quite a few accessories. Vintage transformers however, such as the big Lionel KW and ZW models from the 1950s and 1960s, are powerful but much less efficient than today's solid-state units. Although the older ZWs are rated at 250 or 275 watts, the net output to trains and accessories is quite a bit less.

Smaller modern transformers, such as those rated at 100 watts are efficient but still cannot handle many accessories before becoming overloaded. On a large layout, especially one with a great number of lights, having an auxiliary transformer dedicated to accessories lessens the load on the main transformer.

You can easily tell if you have connected too many units to one transformer. As you turn on more lights, they will dim somewhat, and the trains will run more slowly. Modern transformers have overload protection that trips the circuit breaker and interrupts the power completely.

Use a common ground for the entire layout. Whenever you have two or more transformers on one layout, their ground posts should all be connected together. This saves a considerable amount of wire and results in less confusion when tracing connections to

8

Animated accessories attract lots of attention. In this playground, the merry-go-round goes around, the seesaws tilt, and the swings move.

make repairs. By grounding all of the track and accessories to the same bus wire (explained in Chapter 4), you greatly reduce the number of wires connected to the transformer. Simply connect the ground posts of all of the transformers together.

If all of your transformers are modern, this will work fine. However, if you use vintage transformers or mix vintage with modern, they must all be placed in phase manually. (See Chapter 5, which also shows how to connect two transformers to a single ground bus wire.)

Use an auxiliary transformer for lights. An auxiliary transformer can

power all incandescent bulbs, such as those in buildings, as well as accessories that contain lights. Small bulbs consume a disproportionate amount of power, and a large layout has a surprising number of them. In the area shown in photo **2**, the houses, signal tower, and bank all contain bulbs, and the Lionel hobby shop is brilliantly lit with seven of them. (I started to count the number of bulbs on my layout, and gave up trying when well past 100.) If you must reduce the load, you can replace your incandescent bulbs with modern LED units, but while they consume much less power, they are more expensive.

Adding firemen and vehicles around the MTH House on Fire makes it an even more realistic scene. Because of possible stray droplets, locate this building away from any scenery that might be damaged by water.

An electronic circuit operates the chase lights that create a variety of patterns on the sign for this MTH bus station. Here, the lights are being lit from top to bottom.

Lionel's Ford Auto Dealership is a large two-wire accessory that features two motorized turntables with rotating cars.

Filling the tender with water, pre- and postwar American Flyer style, takes place as a solenoid lowers the spout with the push of a button.

Operate action accessories on the main transformer. Most motorized action accessories will not overload the main transformer (the one used to run trains). The reason for this is simple. When you are operating log or coal loaders, magnetic cranes, and similar accessories, your attention is focused on them and not on the trains, which are usually standing still at that time. This reduces the load on the transformer considerably. There is no reason not to connect this type of accessory to the fixed or variable voltage accessory posts on the main transformer rather than the auxiliary transformer.

Replace accessory switches. In most cases, replace the switches and push buttons that come with accessories with miniature toggle switches

and push buttons from an electronics supply store. This results in a much neater, more compact control panel. The exceptions are any accessories with unusual wiring requirements that have complex control boxes. While it is always possible to replace these controls with generic switches and push buttons, it is often not worth the effort. Unless you have a large number of this type of accessory, a few oversized control boxes shouldn't take up too much room.

Two-wire accessories

All operating accessories require both power and ground connections, and for many of them, this is all that is needed. You simply ground them to the nearest bus wire and run a power wire to a toggle switch or push button on the

control panel and then to the barrier strip connected to an accessory post on the transformer (see Chapter 5).

Figure **3** shows a lamppost wired through a barrier strip to a ZW or Z-4000 transformer. If this is an auxiliary transformer used for accessories only, the track power posts will not be connected to the track. Instead, they can be used as additional variable voltage posts for accessories with differing voltage needs.

If you have several lampposts and buildings with lightbulbs inside, it isn't necessary to run separate wires to each one. Simply connect them all to one power wire, **4**. If lamps and buildings are closer to the bus wire than they are to each other, use separate ground wires as shown at letters A. If

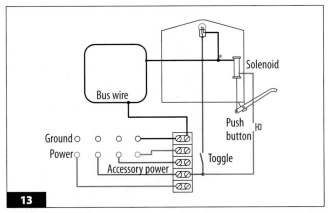

13

Whenever there is power, the bulb stays lit, and the spout only lowers when a button is pushed. The toggle switch turns off the light.

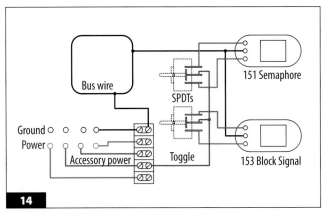

14

These installations, which use an SPDT toggle switch, show how to wire accessories for manual operation.

15

What may be the smallest operating toy trains in the world circle the tracks in Lionel's Mid Town Models hobby shop.

16

Wire connectors masquerade as fire hydrants toward the rear of the hobby shop.

they are closer to each other, connect the ground wires together as shown at letters B.

If you want to control the lampposts and the building lights separately, you will need two toggle switches and two separate power wires, **5**.

There are many two-wire accessories available, such as the Lionel Ice Depot, Lionel Playground, MTH House on Fire, and MTH Greyhound Bus Station. These accessories may be connected in the same manner as the lampposts and buildings, but you will need a separate power wire and switch or push button for each, so they can be operated independently, **6**.

The house on fire, bus station, and playground are connected to the same circuit. As they are meant to operate

continuously, they are also wired through toggle switches.

Lionel Ice Depot. The Lionel Ice Depot consists of an elevated structure with a ramp, on which simulated blocks of ice slide down to a worker holding a long-handled sweeper, **7**. A motor moves the figure toward a refrigerator car, and a metal bar opens the roof hatch on top of the car, so the ice can drop inside. I wired a push button for the Ice Depot so that I can easily control the timing of the delivery of each block of ice. The Ice Depot is wired to one of the track power circuits, which allows an operator to use the throttle handle to control the speed at which the animated worker delivers the ice. The throttle handle on this auxiliary transformer is not used for

track power to run the trains. Almost all two-wire accessories may be wired in this manner.

Lionel Playground. Lionel sells a number of animated scenes like the playground, with its rotating merry-go-round, tilting seesaws, and moving swings, which are activated by magnets in the base, **8**. Other models in the series include carnival midway scenes—a miniature golf game, test-your-strength he-man, pony ride, and tug-of-war. You can also buy two lumberjacks sawing wood and two scenes with a flickering campfire, one surrounded by hobos and the other in which a family enjoys a cookout next to their travel trailer. There's even a gentleman who tips his hat to a lady while his dog irrigates a nearby tree trunk (Mr. Spiff and Puddles), and a man taking a bath in a wooden barrel (Rub-a-Dub-Dub).

MTH House on Fire. The MTH House on Fire is an especially realistic accessory, **9**. It contains a smoke unit, a water pump, and a bulb that glows red to simulate a fire inside. When activated, smoke pours out of the roof and

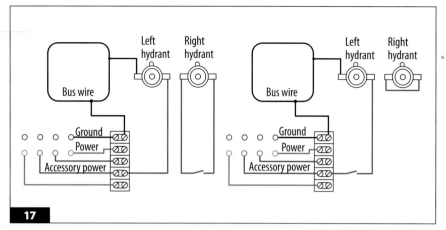

To operate the train layouts, connect a toggle switch to the right fire hydrant posts (at left). To run the trains when the lights are on, connect a jumper wire between the two posts (right).

Raise the roof on this Lionel accessory to watch the tiny barbers at work.

windows, and water flows from the fireman's hose either through the roof or into a window, where it is recirculated back through the hose.

MTH Greyhound Bus Station. Although it contains no moving parts, the MTH Greyhound Station attracts as much attention as any other accessory on my layout because of the animated chase lights on its sign, **10**. The letters light up in ever-changing patterns—top to bottom, bottom to top, from the center outward, one letter at a time, and all letters flashing. Like all of the accessories in this section, it needs only two wires, power and ground, to operate.

Lionel's Ford Auto Dealership. The Ford dealership is a large two-wire accessory that features its own on/off switch, **11**. Having a separate switch is convenient if the accessory is located near the edge of the table, but if it's in the center of the layout or a long way from the control panel, it is not easy to reach. When the two wires (power and ground) are connected, the interior lights are always on. The switch, a rotating fire hydrant, turns on two motorized turntables on which model cars rotate. You can wire this accessory just like any other two-wire unit, with a toggle switch in the power line. If you are willing to have both the lights and the turntables controlled by the toggle switch, you can simply leave the fire hydrant switch turned on all the time.

Three-wire accessories

Three-wire accessories are in the minority, and most feature some form

of action plus a lightbulb that can be wired to stay on constantly. One typical example is the vintage American Flyer Water Tower, which was introduced before World War II and also sold for a few years after the war, **12**. (I received mine for Christmas in 1948.)

A solenoid inside the tower lowers the spout when you push a button, and a lightbulb shines through a plastic lens in the center of the roof to simulate a beacon. When wired according to the instructions, the bulb stays lit whenever there is power present, but the spout only lowers when a button is pushed. Figure **13** shows how this works, with a toggle switch that turns off the light.

Other vintage three-wire accessories that feature both lights and some type of animation (and their reproductions) include the Lionel 356 Freight Station, the 334 Dispatching Board, and the 415 Diesel Fueling Station.

You can also wire some of Lionel's trackside accessories, such as block signals and semaphores, for manual operation. These accessories are usually wired to the track to operate automatically when a train passes by, as explained in Chapter 8. However, if you want to control them manually, connect them as shown in figure **14**.

This installation uses an SPDT toggle switch. For the semaphore, when you throw the switch one way, only the lights come on. When you throw the switch the other way, the semaphore arm descends. For the block signal, throwing the switch one way lights the red bulb. The opposite position of

the switch lights the green bulb. This method of wiring for manual operation may also be used with basic three-wire signals made by other manufacturers.

Four-wire accessories

Some Lionel accessories, such as the Mid Town Models Hobby Shop, have a unique wiring scheme, **15**. The wires are connected to screw-on posts that simulate the arms of two fire hydrants mounted at the back of the building, **16**. This fascinating accessory has a lighted interior and three very tiny operating train layouts that are visible through the front and side windows. When you connect ground and power wires to the two posts on the left fire hydrant, the lights come on.

To operate the mini train layouts, you need a toggle switch connected to the posts of the right fire hydrant, **17**. This arrangement requires a lot of wire if the accessory is far from the control panel. In addition to the power wire from the transformer to the left hydrant, you will need two wires from the toggle switch on the control panel to the right hydrant.

However, if you always expect to operate the miniature trains inside the hobby shop whenever the lights are on, as I do, you can eliminate these last two wires. Just connect a short jumper wire between the two posts of the right hydrant, and put a toggle switch in the power wire from the transformer to the left hydrant. Then, whenever you turn on the toggle, the lights will come on and the tiny trains will circle their layouts.

19

At 14 volts, the figures move across the transfer dock at a realistic speed, but that amount of power makes the lights too bright.

20

Because the two circuits are independent, you can wire the lights at 10 volts and the moving figures at 14 volts.

Harry's Barber Shop is a nicely modeled slice of everyday life, featuring a well-detailed interior, seven figures, a lighted and rotating barber pole outside, and a skylight. The counter in front of the mirror is well stocked with supplies, and there are even two fans suspended from the ceiling.

Unfortunately, the skylight is too small to give a clear view of the action inside, in which the arms of the two barbers swing from side to side as if they are going about their work. Only the tip of one blade on each of the ceiling fans is visible. To thoroughly enjoy this Lionel accessory, you have to lift off the roof, **18**.

Harry's Barber Shop has four connection points for wires: two Fahnestock clips for the power and ground connections and two for an on/off switch. They are located under the floor instead of on fire hydrants. Wiring is exactly the same as the hobby shop. You can follow the manufacturer instructions, in which case the lights are on but the action doesn't begin until you turn on the toggle switch, or add a jumper wire between the two Fahnestock clips for the on/off switch, so the single toggle switch controls both the lights and the action simultaneously.

Independent light circuits

Some four-wire accessories, such as the MTH transfer dock, contain two completely independent circuits, one for the action and one for the lights, **19**. The

21

Large animated accessories, such as the MTH fire station, provide a layout with realistic action. Here, the fire truck leaves the station accompanied by the sounds of a siren and a warning bell.

main advantage of this wiring system is that it allows you to provide different amounts of voltage to the animation and bulbs. The figures move across the open area of the transfer dock at a realistic speed at 14 volts, but with that amount of power, the lights are brighter than you would expect to see in a factory. They look better at about 10 volts. Because the two circuits are independent, you can wire them that way, **20**.

Five-wire accessories

Four large animated accessories from MTH feature complex action and sound. Typical of these toys is the operating fire station, a two-story simulated brick building with large windows and a lighted interior, **21**. At the press of a button, a warning bell sounds, and two red lights over the front door flash alternately. The door

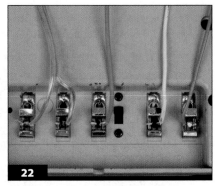

22

Beneath the MTH car wash, the A, B, and C clips (at left) are for power, ground, and the start circuit. The D and E clips at right are for the independent light circuit. The on/off switch is for the smoke unit.

begins to rise while a fireman slides down a pole, visible through a side window. Then a fire truck drives out with siren wailing and turns toward the street. Another push of the button sends the truck backing into the station. The door closes and the fireman goes back up the pole.

The other models are a gas station, a car wash, and Mel's Diner. All four of these accessories employ the same wiring system, consisting of five Fahnestock clips located beneath the base, **22**. The A, B, and C clips are for power, ground, and the start circuit, while the D and E clips are for the independent light circuit. The car wash also contains a miniature slide switch that turns a smoke unit on and off. The smoke simulates steam rising from the wash bay.

The MTH instruction booklet provides the wiring diagram shown at

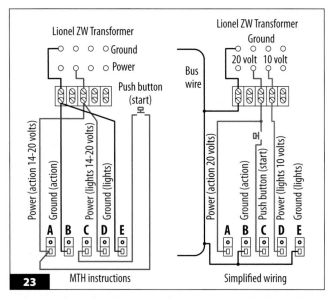

With two independent circuits, one for action and one for lights, you can provide different voltage amounts to the animation and the bulbs.

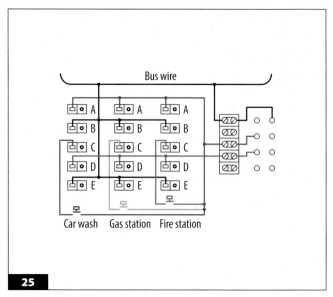

When installing two or more large accessories, you can connect them in parallel, which saves wire.

MTH decorated the car wash (left) to match the colors of the Sinclair gas station at right. Other brand names and color schemes are available for these operating accessories.

left in figure **23**. It works fine, but it requires more wire than is absolutely necessary. Notice especially the length of the two wires leading to the start push button, which are needed if you locate the button on the control panel. Shown at right is a more logical method that eliminates one of the wires to the control panel and shortens the ground wires considerably by connecting them to a bus wire.

The manufacturer recommends using 14–20 volts of power to operate these accessories. If 20 volts are used, the lights appear unrealistically bright.

This method provides a second circuit with less voltage so the lights are softer. On a Lionel ZW Transformer, for example, you can set one of the accessory circuits for 20 volts for action and the other to 10 volts for the lights.

The car wash and gas station look good when located next to each other on a busy highway. When you push the button to start the car wash, a 1950 Ford pulls forward to the window and is greeted by a cheerful attendant, **24**. After a short conversation about prices, the driver pulls the car into the building and sounds of washing begin,

accompanied by steam (smoke) from the hot water. If you wire the car wash to a 14-volt circuit, there probably won't be time for the smoke unit to heat up enough for much smoke to appear. At 20 volts, the smoke comes sooner.

Next, the car moves through the rollers and stops at the exit arch, where red lights come on to suggest the drying cycle. The car then proceeds past two animated attendants who polish the car with the rags they are holding and tell the driver to have a nice day.

The overhead door in the gas station rises, and a 1957 Chevrolet Bel Air coupe drives forward over a simulated chime wire that dings twice, once for the front wheels and once for the back, **24**. The car stops at the pump island, and the sounds of gas being delivered while the meter rings are typical of gas stations half a century ago. The car remains at the pumps until you push the start button again, after which it backs into the station and the door closes.

If you own two or more of these large accessories, they may be connected in parallel to save a lot of wire, **25**. (See Chapter 1 for more on parallel circuits.)

The last of these large accessories is an interpretation of the famous Mel's Diner, complete with 1950s-era carhops on roller skates, **26**. Pushing the start button brings a '57 Chevy Bel Air around from the rear of the building to park in a drive-up slot. A carhop

26

Mel's Diner from MTH features a moving vehicle, roller-skating car hops, and good ol' rock 'n' roll.

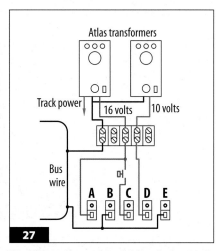

27

The left transformer's variable voltage post is at 16 volts to run the action, and the variable voltage post of the second transformer (right) is at 10 volts for the lights.

skates out, takes the customer's order, and returns to the building as another carhop emerges to take an order from another customer. (On my layout, he's sitting in a vintage Cadillac.) The action is accompanied by the sound of the Chevrolet's engine, an early rock 'n' roll tune, and lots of conversation between the carhops and customers. The sequence concludes with the Chevy backing into its original position.

If the transformer you use to run your trains is relatively small, you can use a second independent power source for the lights in these accessories. Figure **27** shows two Atlas transformers wired to the diner in this manner. One transformer (on left) is also used to run the trains, and its variable voltage accessory post is set at 16 volts to power the diner's action. The variable voltage post of the second transformer (at right) is set at 10 volts for the lights. Note that the ground posts of the two transformers are connected together. This does not affect the independent nature of the action and light circuits.

Dedicated control boxes

To create a neat and compact control panel, I advocate replacing the oversized switches and control boxes that come with accessories with miniature toggle switches and push buttons. However, with some accessories it isn't worth the effort. Several such accessories are the American Flyer

28

This postwar American Flyer crane and Gabe the Lamplighter reproduction both have fairly small dedicated control boxes to manage the action, such as the one shown in the inset.

magnetic crane and a recent Lionel reproduction of Flyer's Gabe the Lamplighter, **28**.

The dedicated control box for Gabe is connected to the accessory by a number of very small-gauge wires contained in a single cable of generous length. Unless the accessory is a long distance from the control area of the layout, you won't need to splice all of the individual wires, and probably won't want to spend the time to disconnect the cable for the sake of substituting miniature push buttons. The relatively small control box does

not take up much room on a control panel, and it is labeled with the name of the accessory for easy identification. Similarly, the control box for the crane is very compact and also labeled.

Manufacturers have achieved an admirable level of scale size and realism in the area of toy train accessories in recent years and have made similar advancements in track. The effort to improve the appearance of traditional tinplate track sections dates back more than seven decades. This is described in Chapter 10 along with wiring conventions that apply to premium brands.

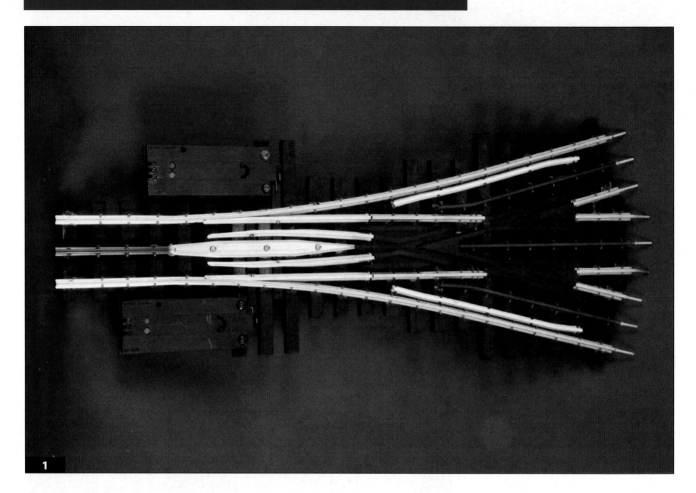

CHAPTER TEN

1

Wiring premium track products

It is possible to model almost any prototype track configuration with today's wide variety of O gauge track products, such as this compact three-way turnout from Ross Custom Switches.

For much of the 20th century, the least realistic component of toy train sets was

the track, with its tubular rails and only three ties on each standard section. While

economical and easy to put together, it hardly resembled prototype rail lines. Today,

there is a wide variety of track products you can use for modeling prototype track, **1.**

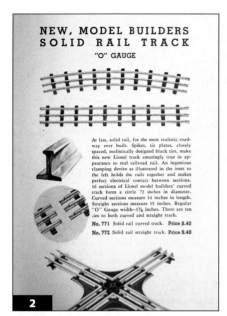

Lionel's designers may have been anticipating the 1937 introduction of its full-scale model of a New York Central Hudson when in 1935 they advertised the first major improvement in track appearance since 1906.

GarGraves (left) and Ross (right) track sections are mounted on realistically spaced wooden ties. GarGraves also makes sections with plastic ties (center).

The undersides of GarGraves and Ross sections are reinforced with plastic (GarGraves) or wooden (Ross) strips that keep the curves in alignment.

The first notable attempt by a major company to create better-looking track appeared in 1935, **2**. With solid T-shaped rails, 10 ties per section, and rail joiners with a passing resemblance to prototype hardware, Lionel's Model Builders Solid Rail Track was a significant step forward. It was a premium product, and the track was marketed in addition to, and not a replacement for, the O gauge and O-27 gauge sectional track products that were the mainstay of the company's business.

Lionel had already begun to move away from toy-like trains with a close-to-scale Union Pacific M-10000 lightweight diesel passenger train and models of the Milwaukee Road's *Hiawatha* and the *Flying Yankee* streamliner. These were major advances in realistic toy train railroading. But just over the horizon was the company's most significant product in the pre-World War II years, a full-scale model of a New York Central Hudson locomotive. Such a magnificent engine could hardly be expected to look good on tubular hollow-rail track.

Model Builders track did not survive the war years and never

reappeared. It was left to an independent manufacturer to champion the movement toward more realistic track, and in 1940, Earle A. Gardner and Eldyn S. Graves developed a product that is still a mainstay of the hobby. GarGraves track consists of hollow tinplate T-shaped rails mounted in slots cut into closely spaced wooden ties. The 3-foot-long sections are flexible and can be shaped into curves of varying diameters.

Special adapter pins allow connection to regular O gauge or O-27 rails so that modelers may expand existing layouts without replacing all of their track. These pins also connect the

GarGraves sections to Lionel turnouts and operating track sections. Ever since the 1950s, GarGraves track has been manufactured with a chemically blackened center rail, which helps to disguise the three-rail nature of toy train track. The company has also developed turnouts and a rust-resistant variation with stainless steel rails.

Over the years, the range of GarGraves products has constantly expanded to include uncouplers, operating track sections, and turnouts of various sizes. The company also makes two-rail O gauge, S gauge, 00 gauge, No. 1 gauge, and standard gauge track.

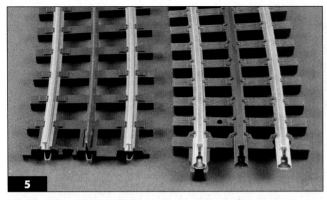

5

MTH ScaleTrax (left) and Atlas O 21st Century track sections have solid T-shaped rails mounted on plastic ties, but there the similarities end.

6

Instead of track pins or rail joiners, ScaleTrax sections (left) have spring-loaded metal contacts that transfer electricity from section to section. Atlas rail joiners (right) are similar to those used for many decades by HO modelers and simulate prototype rail joiners.

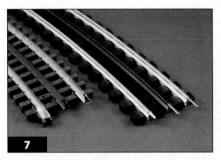

7

Plastic rail joiners (Atlas, left) and pins (GarGraves and Ross, right) insulate an outside rail to operate trackside accessories.

8

To make a insulated ScaleTrax section, pinch the spring connectors on two adjacent rails with a pair of pliers.

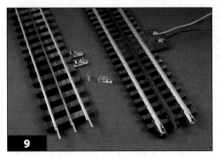

9

This section of GarGraves flexible track (left) is still serviceable after decades of use on my layouts. Fahnestock clips press into slots in the rail bottoms for wiring connections. Atlas makes a terminal track (right) with screw-type connection points for power and ground.

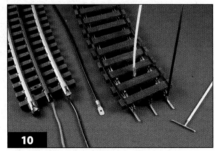

10

Hidden wiring on permanent layouts is made possible with these solutions from Atlas (left) and GarGraves.

A major advancement was the addition of rigid sectional track to the line, **3**. Whereas the flexible product required a certain amount of skill to shape the curves and also to cut them to length, the sectional track made GarGraves products accessible to any modeler who could assemble traditional tinplate track. A very wide range of curve sizes are available today, from a

32" circle (similar to regular O gauge track) to a very wide 138" diameter.

Both the sectional and flexible track products are similarly constructed, with hollow rails inserted in slots in wooden or plastic ties. They connect to one another by means of narrow flat metal pins inserted in the rail ends. The rigid sections are kept in alignment by means of curved plastic strips embedded in the ties underneath, **4**.

In 1972, Ross Custom Switches introduced a line of turnouts and

crossings compatible with GarGraves track. Similar in appearance to the GarGraves product, the Ross track features hollow T-shaped rails spiked to the ties. The line has grown to include many different diameter turnouts and specialty products, such as the three-way model shown in photo **1**. Also available are double crossovers, curved turnouts, wye turnouts, and four-way yard tracks, as well as crossings ranging from 90 degrees to an ultra narrow 11 degrees and very long prototype-style turnouts suitable for large layouts.

More recently, the company has added sectional track in circle diameters from 31" to 128". These sections are similar to the GarGraves product but have individually spiked rails, **3**. All Ross and GarGraves products are fully compatible with each other, and may also be connected to every other make of track through special adapters. The Ross and GarGraves companies cooperate closely, and Ross sells some GarGraves products, such as uncouplers, bumpers for sidings, and flexible track sections.

There are two systems of premium solid rail track on the market, one made by MTH Electric Trains (ScaleTrax) and the other by Atlas O (21st Century), **5**. The MTH product is very low profile, with an unobtrusive narrow middle rail reminiscent of Lionel Super O track from the late 1950s. The rails are held in place by simulated spikes and tie plates molded into the ties. The end ties are shaped

11

This Atlas curved 072/054 model is one of wide variety of specialty turnouts available with switch machines already installed.

12

A moving rod within the core of a twin-coil solenoid is connected to the drawbar. When the SPDT switch is thrown one way, the rod moves to the left and the points move into the straight position (top). When the switch is thrown the other way, the rod moves to the right and the points move to the curved position (bottom).

so as to snap together with adjacent sections. Electrical connection between sections is achieved by means of springy metal contacts, **6**.

The ties on Atlas 21st Century track are approximately the same height as GarGraves and Ross, with simulated spikes and tie plates holding the rails to the ties, **5**. Slip-on rail joiners between sections provide electrical connections. Like the MTH product, the end ties are shaped to snap into adjacent sections, **6**. In addition to rigid curves, both companies make long flexible sections that may be curved to varying diameters.

Trackwork for Toy Trains (Kalmbach Books, 2007) contains comprehensive information about track products from all manufacturers.

Insulated track sections
The outside rails of all brands of premium track are independent of each other. There is no electrical connection between them. This makes it easy to create insulated track sections of any length to operate trackside accessories. Each type of track uses a different method, **7**. Atlas makes a clear rail joiner with a very thin

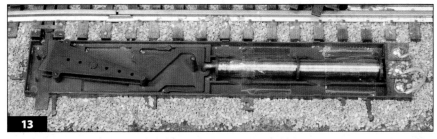

13

Atlas switch machines contain a linear linkage that throws the drawbar. The middle screw at right is the common connection, and the other two screws route power to the solenoid to move the points.

14

A row of Atlas control boxes needs minimal wiring and takes up little room on a control panel. Labels tell the operator which turnout is activated by each switch.

plastic barrier that keeps the rails of adjacent sections apart.

GarGraves sells plastic track pins that also fit Ross track. These pins have one long and one short end, with a slightly raised collar between them that keeps adjacent rails separated. ScaleTrax does not offer an insulated section, but it is easy to make one, **8**. With a pair of pliers, just pinch the spring connectors on

the two adjacent rails so that they do not touch each other.

Remember that you must insulate both ends of the rail. You can make an insulated track any length you need by joining up additional sections between the insulating pins. Keep in mind that you can insulate only one outside rail, however. The opposite rail must always be connected to the ground.

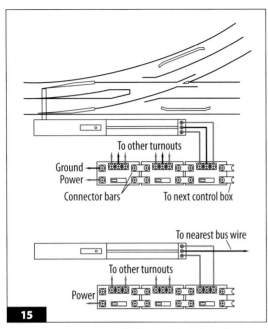

At top are the recommended connections for Atlas turnouts. Green represents the straight position, and red is for curved. You can connect the common post of each turnout to the nearest bus wire of the layout (bottom).

This Atlas under-the-table switch machine adds greater realism, and its drawbar is hidden beneath the pavement for unobtrusive operation.

Power to the track

Track lockons have no counterpart in real railroading, and it is desirable from an aesthetic point of view to have the wiring hidden beneath the track whenever possible. Nevertheless, both Atlas and GarGraves offer ways to connect ground and power wires that are accessible from above. This is especially useful for temporary layouts or on surfaces where it is not possible or desirable to drill holes. The Atlas solution is a straight section of track fitted with two screws, one for the power wire and one for the ground, **9**.

GarGraves makes a set of three press-fit metal bars equipped with Fahnestock clips that slide tightly into the slots in the bottom of the track. They also work well with Ross track, and can even be used with traditional O gauge or O-27 tinplate track.

For hidden wiring, Atlas makes rail joiners with wire leads soldered to the underside, **10**. You can also make your own. GarGraves makes a product that the company calls *pigtails*, lengths of wire soldered either to miniature spade connectors or directly to the track pins. The spade connectors slip into the slot in the bottom of a GarGraves or Ross rail.

All of these Atlas and GarGraves products make it possible to conceal the wires between the ties, where they may be hidden by ballast.

MTH makes a ScaleTrax section with wires preconnected to the metal contacts at one end, which makes them invisible when installed on a layout. If you like a do-it-yourself challenge, it is possible to solder leads like these to any section yourself. However, I don't recommend it, as it is very difficult to heat the joint enough for the wires to be secure without melting the plastic ties with heat from the soldering iron. (See page 91 for soldering techiques.)

Turnout mechanisms

Atlas and Ross Custom Switches produce premium turnouts that are operated by remote control by a switch machine, **11**. These machines are removable and may be placed in a variety of positions next to the turnouts and, in some cases, next to adjacent sections of track. With one notable exception, all of these devices operate the same way. They have an electronic circuit that moves the drawbar of the turnout back and forth. These machines require just three wire con-

nections, one for common and one each for straight and curved. (The exception is the Tortoise slow motion machine described starting on page 88.)

Figure **12** is a schematic representation of a generic switch machine mechanism. A moving rod within the core of a twin-coil solenoid is connected to the drawbar of the turnout. The solenoid coils are wired to the transformer through a spring return-to-center SPDT switch.

When the switch is thrown one way, it energizes half of the solenoid and moves the rod to the left. The triangular linkage pivots and pulls the drawbar to put the turnout points in the straight position. When the switch is thrown the other way, the rod moves to the right and the linkage pivots to push the drawbar. The points move to the curved position. Each manufacturer has a different type of linkage, but they all accomplish the same purpose.

Atlas turnouts

Inside an Atlas switch machine, a twin-coil solenoid, with its internal metal rod, is attached to a linear linkage that moves the drawbar either straight or curved, **13**. A middle screw at the end is the common wire connection, and the two outer screws flanking it carry current for the straight and curved positions of the track points.

You can use a spring return-to-center SPDT or DPDT toggle switch to activate any of the switch machines described in this chapter. These switches are especially useful when installed on a control panel with a graphic representation of the track plan (see Chapter 6). However, each manufacturer supplies some version of an SPDT switch with each switch machine, and they are relatively compact and take up very little room. Wiring the switches is relatively simple and efficient. For example, Atlas no. 56 control boxes are designed to be connected together, which means you only have to provide one power wire and one ground wire to operate any number of turnouts, **14**.

Each Atlas control box contains a combination slide switch/push button. To operate the turnout, you slide the switch either left or right, depending upon which way you want the points to move, and then press it. That sends a momentary burst of current to one side of the solenoid to move the points. I recommend that you standardize your connections—for example, right for curved and left for straight. That way you will always know which way a turnout is thrown by the position the switch was in the last time it was operated.

Figure **15** shows how the company recommends connecting these turnouts. In addition to the ground and power wires from the transformer, three wires from each control box go to its corresponding turnout.

As is so often the case with such products, another way to wire Atlas turnouts will save installation time and eliminate extra wire. You can connect the common post of each turnout to the nearest bus wire (ground) of the layout. Connect the power wire from the transformer to the switch machines as shown and eliminate the ground wire. Now you will only have to run two wires from each control box to its turnout.

17

This Atlas control box features two LEDs that continuously show the position of a turnout. The green light indicates straight and the red light curved.

18

When handling solid-state units, such as this Atlas O Non-Derail Circuit Board, it is advisable to first touch something metal to discharge possible static electricity buildup.

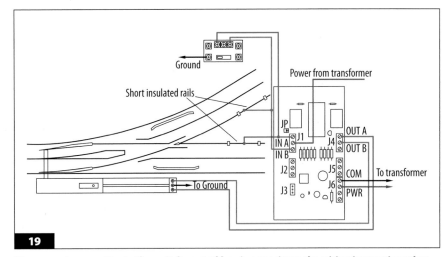

19

The ground connection to the switch control box is opposite to the wiring instructions that come with the Atlas turnouts when using the non-derail circuit board. Also, the control box is wired directly to J1 on the circuit board as shown.

The company makes a switch machine that can be mounted beneath the layout, **16**. With this switch machine, nothing is visible except a wire that sticks up through the hole in the drawbar. Even the drawbar is hidden beneath the pavement, where an above-board switch machine would have blocked the street adjacent to the track. If you plant a small shrub over the drawbar area, nothing will show.

Atlas also makes a lighted control box (no. 57) fitted with two LEDs that show the position of the turnout at all times (green for straight and red for curved), **17**. A lever selects the desired position, and a separate push button

activates the turnout. Atlas switch machines may be mounted on either side of the turnout, facing in either direction.

Most commercial turnouts, such as those from Lionel FasTrack and MTH RealTrax, contain a non-derailing circuit that automatically throws the turnout when a train approaches from the curved or straight side. Although Atlas turnouts do not come with such a circuit, the majority of them, the larger diameter ones, are inherently non-derailing since the wheels of a train are able to deflect the points enough when passing through to avoid derailments.

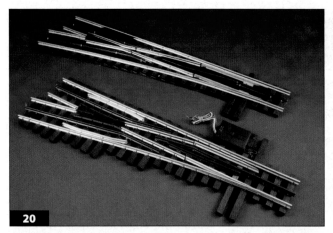

Ross (bottom) and GarGraves (top) turnouts are similar in concept but differ in construction. Ross rails are spiked to wooden ties, while GarGraves attaches them to a molded plastic base. A DZ-2500 switch machine is mounted on this Ross turnout, while the GarGraves manual turnout is ready for the installation of any commercial switch machine.

At right, the DZ-1000 switch machine came from my layout, where it has been in service for almost a decade. It operates with two push buttons, and the control box contains red and green LEDs to indicate turnout position. At left, a single push button manages the electronic circuitry of this DZ-2500 model.

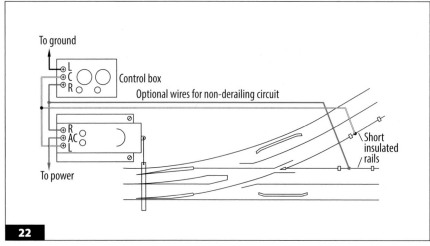

The color-coded wires that come with this machine are black for ground, green for the straight position of the points, and white for the curved position.

Ross and GarGraves turnouts

GarGraves and Ross turnouts are available in manual versions and with Z-Stuff for Trains switch machines already installed, **20**. There are two types of Z-Stuff machines, the model DZ-1000 and the DZ-2500, a more compact version with extra features, **21**. They may be mounted on either side of a turnout.

Both DZ-1000 and DZ-2500 machines come with small push-button controllers that take up little room on a control panel. They are lighted to show the position of the points. Each mechanism is connected to a turnout's drawbar with a semi-rigid spring linkage. The company offers different types of springs for use with almost any brand of turnout.

Both switch machines need only three wires for connection to the control box. Figure **22** shows the basic wiring scheme for the DZ-1000 machine as well as optional wiring for non-derailing operation using short insulated track sections.

The DZ-2500 Switch Machine is a sophisticated device that features slow-speed operation. It may be operated by the push button that comes with it or directly from TMCC or DCS command control handheld remotes. Installation is very simple. Three wires (red, white, and black) connect the switch machine to the control box, **23**.

However, some lightweight cars may not have enough mass to accomplish this, and the linkage of some of the smaller turnouts is somewhat stiff and resists being deflected. To solve this problem, Atlas makes a Non-Derail Circuit Board that not only works with Atlas turnouts but may also be adapted to other manufacturers' products, **18**.

This device may be connected to any conventional three-wire switch machine. It operates in conjunction with an insulated outside rail, **19**. (You may have to reverse the two wires going from Out A and Out B, depending upon which way the switch machine is mounted on the turnout.)

It also contains circuits for a wide variety of options. For example, it can be made to control block signals and other accessories, light turnout indicators on a control panel, and control slow motion machines. It is designed for easy connection to the Atlas 21st Century Signal System (Chapter 8), and is fully compatible with both Lionel TMCC and MTH DCS command control systems. These options are beyond the scope of this book, but Atlas provides clear instructions for their installation. These instructions are also available at the Atlas website (atlaso.com) under New Products, Manuals & Instructions.

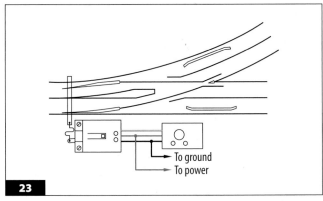

23

Three wires connect the switch machine to the control box. Power from the transformer is also connected to the red wire, and the black wire is grounded. You can attach the black wire of the switch machine to a bus wire.

24

This wiring scheme provides faster operation in non-derail mode. Connect the yellow wire to a short insulated track section on the straight side of the turnout and connect the green wire to an insulated track on the curved side.

Power from the transformer is also connected to the red wire, and the black wire is grounded. (You can attach the black wire of the switch machine to a bus wire.) The other wires (blue, green, and yellow) are not needed for basic operation.

A single button on the control box selects the positions of the points alternately. It takes about 2 seconds for the points to move, but if you wish to have an automatic non-derailing circuit, the turnout needs to move more quickly. Otherwise a fast-moving locomotive would reach the points before they change position.

Figure **24** shows an alternate wiring scheme that allows for faster operation in non-derail mode. Connect the yellow wire to a short insulated track section on the straight side of the turnout and connect the green wire to an insulated track on the curved side.

The non-derailing action will be slow when first installed, as the circuit has to learn the new arrangement. You will have to operate the switch machine a number of times in each direction for the circuit to make this adjustment. Start with the turnout in the curved position. Place a piece of rolling stock on the straight side and move it onto the insulated track. The points will move slowly to the straight position. Push the car away and return the turnout to curved and repeat. It will take about 10 repetitions for the switch machine to reach maximum speed. Then perform the same steps on the curved side of the turnout.

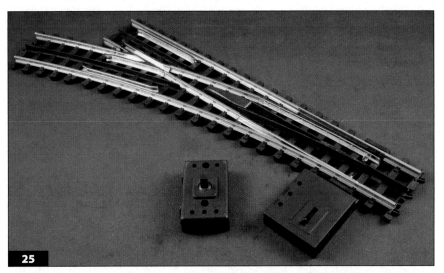

25

ScaleTrax turnouts come in curved models to match 072, 054, and 031 diameter circles, and also in no. 4 and no. 6 versions that approximate the appearance of prototype turnouts. The switch machines are compact and may be mounted on either side. A small control box is included with each turnout.

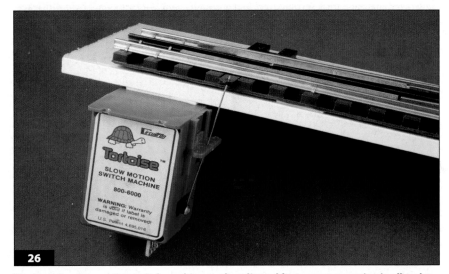

26

The Tortoise slow motion switch machine can be adjusted for turnout operation in all scales, from tiny N gauge to standard or No. 1 gauge. It is shown here connected to an O gauge GarGraves drawbar.

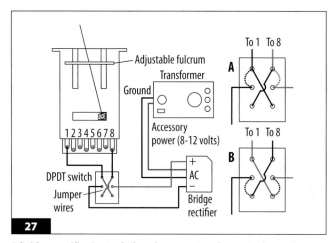

27

A bridge rectifier is needed to change a transformer's alternating current to direct current. A DPDT spring-return-to-center toggle switch controls the operation.

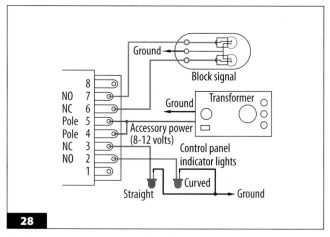

28

Accessory power connects to the poles. The green bulbs are wired to the NC contacts, the straight position of the turnout, and the red bulbs are wired to the NO contacts, the curved position.

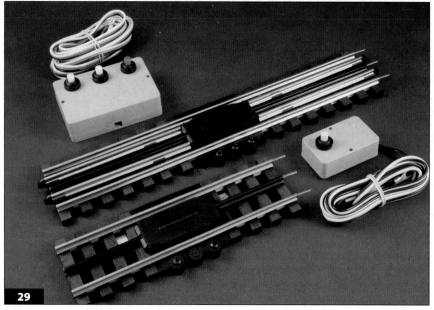

29

GarGraves operating track sections (top) and uncouplers (bottom) are compatible with track made by Ross Custom Switches.

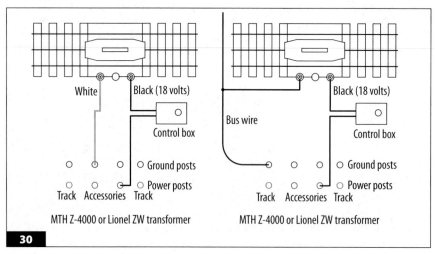

30

To simplify the wiring, remove the white ground wire (shown at left) and connect the left-hand screw on the uncoupler to the nearest bus wire (right).

Z-Stuff for Trains switch machines may be used with Atlas, Ross, and GarGraves turnouts. Advanced modelers and those using TMCC or DCS command control systems may wish to take advantage of the other features offered by these devices. (More information may be found at z-stuff.net.)

ScaleTrax turnouts

MTH makes five different sizes of turnouts in the ScaleTrax line: 072, 054, 031, no. 4, and no. 6. Each comes with a dedicated switch machine and control box, **25**. No additional wiring is required, as the machine draws power directly from the track. The low-profile switch machine may be mounted on either side of a turnout to accommodate space restrictions. An SPDT spring return-to-center toggle switch or two normally open push buttons may be substituted for the control box.

ScaleTrax turnouts do not require an electronic non-derailing circuit. The movable points are designed so that the wheels of a passing train can deflect them easily. Once the train's wheels have cleared the turnout, the points return to their original position.

Tortoise slow motion switch machines

Designed to mount below a layout, Tortoise switch machines offer slow motion operation and a built-in capability for operating block signals and control panel indicator lights, **26**.

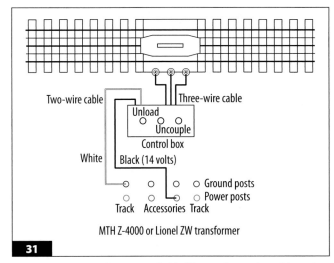

31

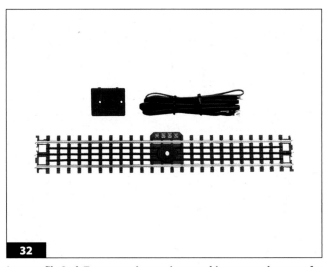

32

The control box has five wires, divided into a three-wire cable and a two-wire cable, which is for power (black) and ground (white).

Low-profile ScaleTrax operating sections combine a central magnet for uncoupling with control rails for operating cars. *Photo courtesy MTH.*

Since they were originally designed for use on scale model railroads, most of which require direct current (DC) for operation, the mechanism operates on DC only. They are manufactured by Circuitron (www.circuitron.com) and are available from other distributors.

A miniature reversible motor swings a stiff wire back and forth to move the turnout drawbar. The range of motion is adjusted by moving a fulcrum up and down, and the motor generates plenty of torque to close the points completely. For AC-powered trains, the basic wiring requires a bridge rectifier to change a transformer's alternating current to direct current, **27**. A DPDT spring return-to-center toggle switch controls the action.

The power and ground wires from the transformer connect to the two inner AC connections of the bridge rectifier. The two outer wires of the rectifier are the plus (+) and minus (-) DC output. Connect these to the poles of the DPDT switch. The motor of the switch machine (posts 1 and 8) connects to the end contacts of the DPDT. You must also install two jumper wires between these end contacts of the DPDT to the contacts at the opposite end of the switch, right to left and left to right.

At letter A, the schematic diagram of a DPDT shows how the switch works. One position of the handle connects the plus (red) and minus (black) poles of the DPDT to the upper contacts,

indicated by the dotted lines. Plus goes to 8 on the switch machine, and minus goes to 1 to operate the motor.

At letter B, the switch has been thrown the other way, and current from the poles travels to the lower contacts of the DPDT, then through the jumper wires to the upper contacts, and on to the switch machine. But now, the plus and minus aspects of the current are reversed, with plus going to 1 and minus going to 8. The DC motor in the switch machine reverses direction according to which way the current passes through it.

The Tortoise switch machine contains two internal SPDT switches that change position when the motor operates, **28**. Each one has a pole and two contacts, normally open (NO) and normally closed (NC). They may be connected to operate a block signal, a pair of indicator lights on a control panel to show the turnout position, or almost any other two- or three-wire trackside accessory.

Accessory power connects to the poles (contacts 4 and 5), and the green bulbs are wired to the NC contacts (3 and 6) to correspond to the straight position of the turnout. The red bulbs are wired to the NO contacts (2 and 7), which close when the motor moves the turnout to the curved position. (You may have to reverse the NC and NO wiring, depending upon which way the switch machine is aligned under the layout.)

Uncouplers and operating track sections

GarGraves uncoupling and operating track sections are mounted on wooden ties and come with dedicated control boxes. The 107 Uncoupler has a central magnet and two wire connection points, ground and accessory power, **29**. Two black wires extend from the controller, with a white wire unconnected at both ends.

Unlike the more common practice in model railroading, where ground wires are usually black, the white wire supplied by GarGraves is the ground connection, and the black wire receives accessory power from the transformer.

A simplified method using a layout's bus wire shows black for power, **30**. Eliminate the white wire and connect the left-hand screw on the uncoupler to the nearest bus wire. Although the control box is quite small, you may wish to replace it with a miniature push button on a graphic control panel.

Pushing the button energizes the magnet to open the couplers on a train. The company also makes a compact version less than 3" long (no. 117).

The no. 108 Operating Track Section also has a central magnet, plus control rails similar to the Lionel and MTH products, to control operating cars, **29**. There are three connection points for wires. The three-button control box has five wires,

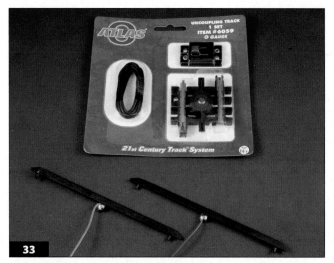

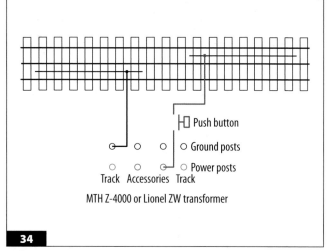

33 Atlas uncouplers (top) are very short to allow installation almost anywhere on a layout. For operating cars, two control rails (bottom) may be installed on any straight section of track.

34 Wiring is simple when you use a miniature push button on a control panel. One rail is grounded (black wire) and the other is connected to accessory power (blue wire).

35 Atlas control rails are unobtrusive when installed in a section of ballasted track. They may also be installed on the ties of GarGraves and Ross track sections.

divided into a three-wire cable and a two-wire cable. The three-wire cable connects to the track section, **31**. The two-wire cable is for power (black) and ground (white).

To uncouple cars, push both the center (yellow) and right (red) buttons simultaneously. To activate an operating car, push the center and left (white) buttons at the same time. This unit is also made with the magnet located at one end (no. 108-EM).

The MTH ScaleTrax operating track section also has a dedicated control box, **32**. There are four wire connections between the box and the track and a central magnet for uncoupling. This section is a full 15" long, allowing plenty of latitude when locating accessories next to it. MTH does

not offer a separate uncoupler in the ScaleTrax line.

Atlas uncoupler magnets are mounted in a very short section of track, **33**. To install one, you need to connect a wire from an accessory post, providing about 14 volts, to the track through the push button that comes with the unit or a miniature push button of your choice. The magnet is grounded to the track, so no separate ground wire is required.

Unlike most other manufacturers, Atlas does not make a special operating track section. Instead, the company offers two individual control rails that may be installed in any section of straight track anywhere on a layout. Two studs on each control rail are inserted in holes in the ties to

keep them in place. Atlas molds locations for the holes in the underside of straight sections. They must be drilled out to accept the studs. You can also drill extra holes in ties where these molds do not exist. A third stud in the middle of each rail is threaded for a screw to attach a wire.

Wiring is very simple, using the push-button control box that comes with the rails or any miniature push button on a control panel, **34**. One rail is grounded while the other is connected to accessory power (12–14 volts). You can mount these rails independently or on either side of an Atlas uncoupling magnet track section, **35**.

Atlas control rails may be placed anywhere you wish to have an operating car unload its cargo. You can drill holes in the ties from above to receive the mounting studs without having to take up any of the track. Atlas control rails may also be mounted on Ross or GarGraves track sections. Be sure to center them exactly between the outer and middle rails. If the grounded control rail is placed too near to the middle rail, pickup rollers on locomotives and cars may touch it and cause a short circuit.

Chapter 8 discussed the use of electronic relays to make automatic trackside accessories operate realistically. In Chapter 11, we will use these relays to add a dimension of automatic control to the trains themselves.

Soldering techniques

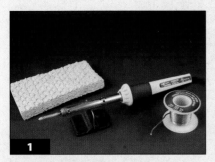

1

To make electrical solder connections, you will need a 30- or 35-watt soldering iron along with rosin-core solder, a stand, and a sponge. Keeping the soldering iron in the stand prevents any accidental damage.

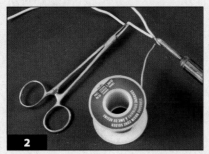

2

If you hold wires in a hemostat while soldering, they will not move. Good tools last a lifetime or longer. I remember seeing my father use this hemostat when building a high fidelity amplifier to play long-playing microgroove records that came out in 1947.

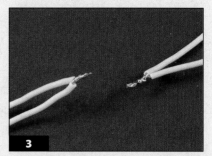

3

The secret to good soldered joints is to heat the surfaces to be joined so the solder melts when it touches them. A good joint is smooth and shiny (left), with a minimum of extra solder coating the wires. A cold joint will appear grainy or lumpy (right).

4

Let the solder flow into the joint from the side of the wire that is opposite to the iron's tip. This GarGraves track has wooden ties, which are not affected by heat in the rails.

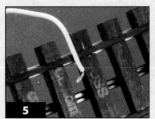

5

Since solder will not stick to the black coating on the middle rail of this Ross track section, scrape it off before applying heat. Do this for all track sections with blackened middle rails.

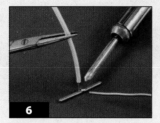

6

When soldering a length of wire to a track pin, keep the joint small so track sections maintain a close connection.

7

Placing Atlas track joiners in a slot cut in a block of wood secures them when soldering wires to them and avoids any damage to the track.

Before beginning to solder any connections, set your soldering iron on its stand and allow it to heat up thoroughly. For soldering wire, a 30- or 35-watt soldering iron and rosin-core solder work best, **1**. Melt a small amount of solder on the tip each time you plug in the iron. Moisten a sponge and use it to clean the tip as you work.

To solder two or more wires, first twist them together tightly. It is advisable to hold them in a hemostat or vise so that they will not move, **2**.

Next, place the hot tip of the iron firmly against the joint for several seconds. Then touch the solder to the joint, not the iron. If the wires have been heated sufficiently, the solder will flow into the joint and bind the wires together, **3**. Hot solder applied to insufficiently heated wires will result in a cold joint, which may not conduct electricity well and will be prone to coming apart.

To solder a stranded wire to the underside of a slotted rail, twist the strands together tightly. Lay the wire laterally against the slot in the bottom of the rail—make sure they are in firm contact. Place the hot tip of the iron against the rail and against the side of the wire. It may take quite a few seconds for the rail to heat up enough to melt the solder. Let the solder flow into the joint from the side of the wire that is opposite to the iron's tip, **4**. Remove the iron and allow the joint to cool before putting any pressure on the joint. (GarGraves track with plastic ties may melt a bit from the heat. To avoid this, remove the iron as soon as the joint has fused.)

When soldering track that has blackened middle rails, such as those from GarGraves and Ross Custom Switches, scrape off the black coating to expose bare metal before applying heat, **5**. The solder will not stick to the coating.

You can also solder wires to GarGraves or Ross track pins, **6**. When making track-pin pigtails, be careful to use the least possible amount of solder and keep the joint as small as possible. Otherwise you won't be able to connect sections of track closely together. You must also be careful when assembling the track not to let the rails disturb the solder joint.

Atlas 21st Century track has plastic ties and solid rails. Do not attempt to solder wires to these rails, **7**. Instead, solder them to the bottom of the rail joiners. Scrape the coating from the bottom of the black joiners that connect the middle rails. Place the joiner in a slot cut in a block of wood to hold it securely, and apply heat to both the joiner and the wire. Touch the solder to the joint on the side of the wire that is opposite to the tip of the iron.

CHAPTER ELEVEN

1

Automatic train control

To operate two trains safely on the same track, your layout should have a relatively long continuous main line. The Chessie freight train (at right) has a heavy load, and the fast passenger train was overtaking it until an independent track block in front of the station stopped the Canadian Pacific diesel long enough for the slower train to open up a bigger lead.

While most operators enjoy the hands-on running of their layout, it can sometimes be fun to see the trains performing on their own, stopping and starting without input from the engineer. Automatic train control makes it possible to run two trains on one track, **1**.

Most transformers are powerful enough to handle two locomotives. However, one of the two locomotives will inevitably be faster than the other, resulting in an eventual rear-end collision. You need a circuit to slow down the faster train for maintaining a safe distance.

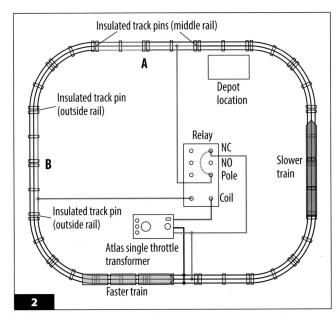

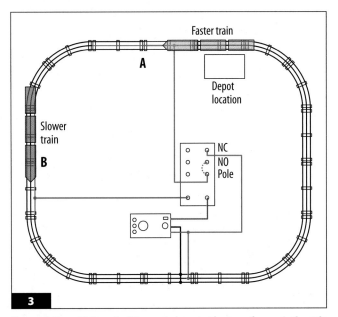

This circuit, with a 12-volt DPDT relay, helps trains maintain safe distance.

Connect the middle rail of the main loop to the transformer's throttle post (red) and connect the outside rails to the ground (black).

Wiring a circuit

You need a circuit to slow down the faster train for maintaining a safe distance. The key to this circuit is a 12-volt DPDT relay made to operate on alternating current (AC).

Refere to Chapters 3 and 9 for information about independent track blocks, insulated rails, and electronic relays. To connect the wires, follow these six steps, as shown in figure **2**:

1. Create an independent block (at A in the diagram) by insulating the middle rail of two or more track sections.
2. Several track sections ahead of this block, install at least two sections with an insulated outside rail at B.
3. Connect the middle rail of the loop to the throttle post of the transformer (red) and connect the outside rails to the ground (black), **3**.
4. Connect the NC contact of a 12-volt AC electronic relay to the same throttle post.
5. Connect the pole of the relay to the middle rail of the independent block.
6. Connect the coil of the relay to a fixed or variable voltage post providing about 12–14 volts (blue wire) and also to the insulated outside rail (green wire).

If you use a DC relay fitted with a bridge rectifier instead of an AC relay, follow figure **4**.

In order for this sequence to work properly, you must set the reverse unit of the faster locomotive to forward-only operation. Otherwise when the power comes back on in the independent block, the train will be left standing in neutral.

To understand how this circuit works, imagine two trains traveling counter-clockwise on the loop, with the faster train beginning to catch up with the slower one. When the slower train enters the independent block (A), it continues to run because that track receives power from the normally closed contact of the relay (indicated by the dashed line between the pole and NC contact), **2**. When the slower train reaches the insulated sections (B), it activates the relay, which turns off the power to the independent block (A) because the pole is now connected to the NO contact (dashed line), **3**. When the faster train reaches the independent block (A), it stops beside the station because no current is reaching the middle rail.

As the slower train continues forward, it leaves the insulated track (B), which turns off the relay, **5**. This restores power to the middle rail of the isolated block (A), and the faster train begins to move again. The slower train has now moved some distance away, and the two trains will continue to run

until the faster one again catches up enough for the cycle to repeat itself.

If you have a transformer with two throttles, such as an MTH Z-4000 or a Lionel ZW, you don't have to turn off the reverse mechanism of the faster train, **6**. You can preserve the train's reversing capability by making the following connection changes:

1. Connect the middle rail of the main part of the loop to the Track 1 throttle post of the transformer (red) to be operated by the right-hand throttle.
2. Also connect the NC contact of the relay to the Track 1 throttle post.
3. Connect the NO contact of the relay to the Track 2 throttle post (purple). All other wiring remains the same.

Set the Track 2 throttle to a lower voltage than the Track 1 throttle. Now when the slower train is on the insulated track (B), the relay will connect the independent block (A) to the second throttle. The train will slow down instead of stop, and the reverse unit will not operate. As soon as the slower train leaves the insulated track, the faster train will speed up again. You can still have the faster train stop at the station by setting the second throttle to the lowest possible voltage, enough to keep the reverse unit from operating but not enough to let the locomotive's motor run.

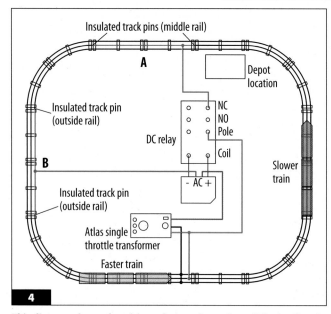

4

This diagram shows the wiring scheme when using a DC relay fitted with a bridge rectifier instead of an AC relay.

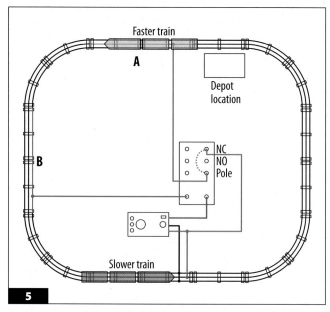

5

As the slower train leaves the insulated track (B), it turns off the relay, restoring power to the isolated block (A), and the faster train moves.

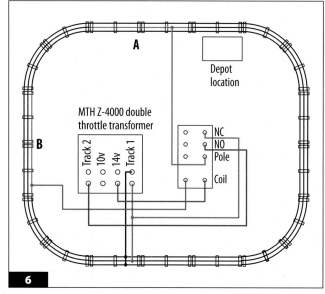

6

To preserve the train's reversing capability, make these wiring changes when using a double-throttle transformer.

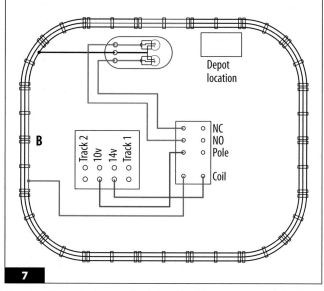

7

Connect the track wires to the right-side relay contacts and the block signal wires to the left side. (Track wiring is omitted for clarity.)

Automatic signal lights

To increase the realism of two-train operation, you can install a block signal that faces the approaching traffic. With the track wires connected to the right-side contacts of the relay, attach the block signal wires to the left side, **7**. When the slower train causes the faster train to slow down, the signal will turn red, as if it were warning the faster train's engineer of danger ahead. Follow these four steps to wire the block signal:

1. Ground the block signal to the track, to a bus wire, or to the transformer, whichever is most convenient.
2. Connect the left pole of the relay to an accessory post suitable for lights, such as the 10-volt post on a Z-4000 Transformer.
3. Connect the left NC contact of the relay to the green bulb of the block signal.
4. Connect the left NO contact of the relay to the red bulb of the block signal.

When no train is on the insulated track (B), the relay is off, and the green bulb of the block signal will light. When the slower train enters the insulated track and the faster train approaches the signal, the relay is activated, and the red bulb comes on as the faster train slows down.

Modern electronics make it possible to install sophisticated automatic train control circuits on a layout. Those interested in such circuits should investigate the products made by Dallee Electronics (dallee.com).

About the author

Peter Riddle has devoted his professional life to education. Following eight years of teaching in the public schools of New Jersey and Nova Scotia, he joined the faculty of Acadia University, where his responsibilities included the preparation of teachers. He served for a decade as Director of the Acadia School of Music, and he continues to teach part-time since his partial retirement in 2005.

His publications include musical compositions and arrangements, eight novels, two novelettes for young readers, a children's picture book, and 14 books about model railroading, the majority of an instructional nature. His first article for *Classic Toy Trains* magazine was included in the second issue, and since then, his byline has appeared more than 75 times.

Peter's wife Gay contributes her editing skills and knowledge about toy trains to his hobby-related books. They make their home in Nova Scotia and have two children and three grandchildren.

Sources

Train set manufacturers
Atlas O: atlaso.com
Lionel: www.lionel.com
MTH Electric Trains: mthtrains.com
Williams by Bachmann: www.bachmanntrains.com

Locomotive and rolling stock manufacturers
3rd Rail (Sunset Models): 3rdrail.com
ETS (Electric Trains Systems): ets-trains.com
Ready Made Toys (RMT): readymadetoys.com
Schneider Model Railroading (SMR Trains): smrtrains.com
Weaver Models: weavermodels.com

Specialty track manufacturers
GarGraves Trackage: www.gargraves.com
Ross Custom Switches: www.rossswitches.com

Accessory manufacturers
Circuitron: www.circuitron.com
Dallee Electronics: dallee.com
NJ International: njinternational.com
Z-Stuff for Trains: z-stuff.net

Electronics parts suppliers
George Tebolt Train Parts: georgetebolt.com
J&K Trains & Parts: jktrains.com
J and W Electronics: jandwelectronics.com
Stan Orr Train Parts: stanorrtrainparts.com
Town & Country Hobbies: towncountryhobbies.com

Dedication

My books about model railroading could not have been written without the untiring help and support of one very important person. Her knowledge of the hobby, expertise with language, and long hours of patient work proofing the manuscripts made my work immeasurably easier. And so this book is especially for Gay Riddle, my best friend, professional partner, and wife for more than 50 years.

Acknowledgements

The author is indebted to the following companies and individuals for their kind assistance and/or donation of products used in the preparation of this book:

Atlas O: Jerry Kimble
GarGraves Trackage: Michael Roder
Lionel
MTH Electric Trains: Andy Edelman
Ross Custom Switches: Steve Brenneisen and Tom Monroe
Toy Train Workshop: Tom Bellfoy
Z-Stuff For Trains: Dennis R. Zander

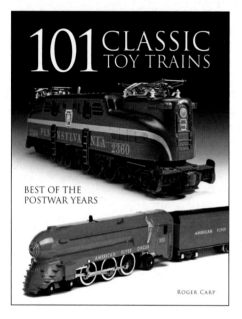
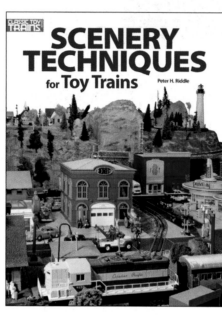
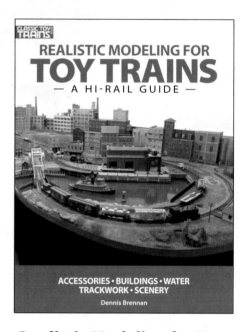